JOHN STEINBECK
A WRITER'S LIFE

JOHN STEINBECK

A WRITER'S LIFE

JOHN TESSITORE

FRANKLIN WATTS
A Division of Scholastic Inc.
New York/Toronto/London/Auckland/Sydney
Mexico City/New Delhi/Hong Kong
Danbury, Connecticut

To my wife Kelly,
who has made a habit of helping people

Photographs ©: Archive Photos: 124 (Agence France Presse), 42 (American Stock), 46 (Metro-Goldwyn-Mayer), 97 (Irving Newman), 3 (Popperfoto), cover foreground, 51, 69, 71, 103, 105; Brown Brothers: cover background; Corbis-Bettmann: 16 (Philip James Corwin), 10, 64, 117; National Archives at College Park: 122 (Abbie Rowe); National Steinbeck Center, Salinas, CA: 19; Stanford University Libraries: 33 (Department of Special Collections); Valley Guild-Steinbeck House, Salinas, CA: 15, 17, 93, 127.

Interior design by Vicki Fischman

Visit Franklin Watts on the Internet at:
http://publishing.grolier.com

Library of Congress Cataloging-in-Publication Data

Tessitore, John
John Steinbeck, a writer's life / by John Tessitore
p. cm.
Includes bibliographical references and index.
ISBN 0-531-11707-3
Steinbeck, John, 1902-1968—Juvenile literature. 2. Novelists, American—20th Century—Biography—Juvenile literature. [1. Steinbeck, John, 1902-1968. 2. Authors, American. 3. Nobel Prizes—Biography.] I Title.

PS3537.T3234 Z896 2001
813'.52—dc21
[B] 00-038200

Printed in the United States of America
1 2 3 4 5 6 7 8 9 10 R 09 08 07 06 05 04 03 02 01

CONTENTS

JOHN
STEINBECK
A WRITER'S LIFE

INTRODUCTION

You are the perfect knight of now and then and of a thousand unhatched years. Men will know your deeds written with your sword, but they will ask, "What was he like?"

—*from* The Acts of King Arthur and His Noble Knights[1]

ON DECEMBER 10, 1962, John Steinbeck stood before the Swedish Academy in Stockholm to accept the Nobel Prize for Literature, the most prestigious award in world letters. He hated public speaking but now he filled the spotlight, a large, sixty-year-old man proud of his accomplishments as a writer. "Literature is as old as speech," he growled, looking out at a hall full of scholars and dignitaries. "It grew out of human need for it, and it has not changed except to become more needed . . . [W]riters are not separate and exclu-

John Steinbeck receives the 1962 Nobel Prize for Literature from Sweden's King Gustav Adolf in Stockholm.

sive. From the beginning, their fictions, their duties, their responsibilities have been decreed by our species."[2]

As he explained that day, John Steinbeck believed that literature was a necessity of human life; at its best, it revealed injustices and gave people hope, and Steinbeck struggled to accomplish these things in his own work. When he wrote well, the world read his words. His masterpiece, *The Grapes of Wrath*, became one of the most important books of the twentieth century. Other novels, such as *Of Mice and Men*, *Tortilla Flat*, and *East of Eden*, made him world famous. In all of these works, Steinbeck explored the major issues of his day, and of any day—greed and corruption, friendship and loyalty, fear and survival, weakness and heroism—and he found his way into the hearts of past and future readers.

As much as he craved popularity, however, Steinbeck hated the publicity and celebrity that came to writers in the age of radio and television. "The business of being a celebrity has no reference to the thing I am interested in. And that is my work," he once told a reporter. "Also, it's nobody's damn business how I live."[3] For Steinbeck, the work was most important. But, through his work, he sought to make himself a better person and to make others better as well.

This, then, is the story of a celebrity and a writer, an observer and a leader, a hero and an ordinary man.

CHAPTER ONE
SALINAS

"For ten months you will train and learn," she said. "And then, I promise you, you will have more adventures and more profitable ones than the others in twelve months."

—*from* The Acts of King Arthur and His Noble Knights[1]

JOHN STEINBECK was born on February 27, 1902 in Salinas, California, the central town in the Salinas Valley. Primarily a lettuce-growing region, the valley also supported many small ranches, pastures, and canneries. Peopled with farmers, migrant laborers, and the speculators who recognized California's potential as an agricultural and industrial center, Salinas was more than a home to young John. It was a mythical, almost enchanted, setting, a small paradise created by his ancestors.

John's paternal grandfather, John Adolph Grosssteinbeck, helped to establish Salinas. Born near Düsseldorf, Germany, Grosssteinbeck was a cabinetmaker until 1852, when he and his family traveled to Jerusalem to join a Lutheran mission. There, he fell in love with and married Almira Dickson, the daughter of an American missionary. Soon after their wedding, John Adolph and Almira fled an outbreak of violence in Jerusalem, returned to the Dickson family home in Massachusetts, and changed their name to "Steinbeck." Later, they moved to Florida, where the Confederate army drafted John Adolph to fight in the Civil War. He eventually deserted the army, fled to Florida, and, ten years later, led his growing family west to California in covered wagons. They settled on ten acres in the Salinas Valley, where John Adolph raised cows and fruit trees, ran a flour mill, and lived a comfortable life.

Samuel Hamilton, John's maternal grandfather, would figure even more prominently in John's later work. Born in Northern Ireland, Hamilton left the old country for the United States when he was seventeen years old. He married an American girl of Irish ancestry, Elizabeth "Liza" Fagen, in New York in 1849, and the newlyweds set out separately for California in 1850. Samuel sailed around Cape Horn and Liza sped across the Isthmus of Panama, a journey that would fire John's imagination and inspire his first novel, *Cup of Gold.* After living for twenty years in San Jose, the Hamiltons moved to Salinas, where Samuel signed the city charter as a founding settler. Despite his prominence in the new town, Samuel grew restless in Salinas and bought a homestead near King City, forty-five miles southeast of Salinas. The new land was too dry to farm so Samuel served as the region's blacksmith and worked as an amateur inventor. Somehow he sustained his family of nine children and sent his daughter Olive to Salinas for teacher training.

By the time she was eighteen, Olive Hamilton was teaching all grades in a Monterey schoolhouse. Not long after she began teaching, she married John Ernst Steinbeck, the quiet son of John Adolph. The newlyweds moved back to Salinas, where John Ernst became the manager of a large flour mill. Unlike their parents, pioneers in the westward expansion of the United States, Olive and John Ernst settled into a conventional lifestyle devoid of adventure or excitement.

John Steinbeck, the writer, would remember his father as a man who could never fulfill his own dreams.

John Steinbeck's parents, John Ernst (left) and Olive (right)

"I remember his restlessness," Steinbeck later wrote. "It sometimes filled the house to a howling although he did not speak often."[2] During John Ernst's tenure as manager, the flour mill closed. His next venture, a horse feed store, also failed—partly because he proved to be a poor businessman. Running out of options, he ran for Monterey County treasurer, an elected office that promised a steady income and a measure of prominence in the community. Although he disliked politics, John Ernst won the election (and held the position until he died in 1936). He purchased a neat house behind a white picket fence and moved the family to Central Avenue on the prosperous side of Salinas.

A present-day photograph of the Steinbeck family home on Central Avenue in Salinas, California

John was the third Steinbeck child, behind Esther (born in 1892) and Beth (born in 1894), and three years older than Mary. As Olive's only son, he was destined to be a spoiled child, and complications during his birth, and his frail health, only insured that Olive would pamper him for the rest of his life.[3]

Among the most important things the Steinbeck parents taught their children was a respect for the natural landscape. Olive approached the land with a sense of wonder while John Ernst taught the children practical lessons about farming and survival. He raised chickens, hogs, and a cow at the Central Avenue house, and bought his children a Shetland pony named Jill who

This photograph of a young John Steinbeck with his sister, Mary, riding Jill, was taken on August 28, 1907.

would figure prominently in John's later story, "The Red Pony." He also bought a summer cottage in the village of Pacific Grove, an oceanfront community near Monterey. On weekends, the family traveled to the coast, where the children would explore the beaches and tide pools.

Olive and John Ernst had few problems raising their daughters, but their son was a constant source of concern. As one Salinas neighbor remembered, "Mrs. Steinbeck was sometimes in despair about John, trying to get him to achieve more than he did. . . . She often said that he would either go to the White House as president or go to jail."[4] Before he was old enough to attend the Salinas schools, Olive taught her son to read. He devoured books such as *Robin Hood, Treasure Island* and the legends of King Arthur. In one of his favorite books, Robert Louis Stevenson's *Prince Otto,* he scribbled that he wanted to become a writer.[5] Unfortunately, he seemed to prefer the fictional worlds of his favorite authors to real life in Salinas. Awkward in appearance and uncomfortable in public, he hid in his bedroom in the attic of the Central Avenue house, composing stories and daydreaming.

His life improved when he entered high school. After the United States entered World War I in 1917, John and his classmates joined the Student Training Corps, a program designed to prepare high school boys for potential military service. John became junior officer of the group, organizing drills and rifle practice as well as overseeing the students who worked the Salinas bean fields and fruit orchards while the regular workers fought in Europe. Teachers boosted his confidence by encouraging him to develop his writing skills. He even submit-

John Steinbeck (middle row, right) was a forward on the 1919 Salinas Union High School basketball team.

ted a few stories for publication before he graduated high school, though no one accepted this early work.

During his junior year, he contracted pleural pneumonia. Doctors performed emergency surgery to remove a rib and drain the infection from his lungs. In an age before antibiotics, his recovery was slow and painful.

After spending nine weeks in bed, he had to learn how to walk again. But he returned to school in the fall with renewed energy. He was elected senior class president and associate editor of the yearbook, to which he contributed several articles. As he finished his high school career, his parents convinced him to follow in his older sisters' footsteps and enter college. So after working in a carpenter shop that summer, he headed to the brand new Leland Stanford Junior University in Palo Alto, California, known simply as Stanford. As a friend remembered, he was ready for anything: "John left Salinas with a sigh of relief. I don't think it mattered where he was going. Anywhere was better than home."[6]

The new Stanford campus sprawled across a wheat field, an idyllic setting for serious students. But John was more interested in girls, cigarettes, and cheap alcohol than university life. By December, his parents received a letter from the dean of students explaining that John was failing several courses. In the spring, an attack of appendicitis and a serious bout of the flu cut his year short. He completed only three courses in his first year.

He found a job with land surveyors in the Santa Lucia mountains that summer, carrying heavy backpacks up steep, rocky slopes. Then his father found him a less punishing job at the Spreckles sugar plant in Salinas. Spreckles leased ranches and farms all over the Salinas Valley, primarily to grow the beets used to produce sugar. But the company also grew hay and alfalfa and raised cattle. To work the ranches and farms, Spreckles hired itinerant Mexican and Filipino immigrants known as "bindlestiffs." Although John worked as a maintenance man in the main plant, he met many bindlestiffs and heard their stories of life on the road. To a boy who raised himself on the tales of King Arthur and his wandering knights, the bindlestiffs seemed to live romantic lives.

Grudgingly, John left the bindlestiffs to return to Stanford in the fall. He made a halfhearted attempt to survive academic probation and even read some of the books assigned by his professors. But he wrote stories when he should have been studying. And he drank too much red wine. One day, his roommate found a note in their dorm room: "Gone to China. See you again sometime."[7] John made his way to the docks in San Francisco and tried to earn a berth on a ship bound for Asia. But since he had no experience on the high seas, no one would hire him. He spent Christmas with a friend's family in Oakland, earning money by clerking at a department store selling men's clothes, an odd job for someone who cared so little about what he wore.

In early 1921, after hitchhiking back to Salinas, he found a job as a "straw boss," managing a band of bindlestiffs on a Spreckles farm. For four months he lived with his coworkers and learned Spanish so that he could converse with them. He loved the flowery language they used, even while cursing, and he paid them to tell him their stories. After his crew finished picking the beet crop, he worked as a bench chemist at a Spreckles laboratory and moved back to Central Avenue. To satisfy his mother, he reapplied to Stanford in 1923 and was accepted once again.

His third stay in Palo Alto was perhaps his happiest. He roomed with Carlton "Dook" Sheffield, a young man who had almost as many opinions about literature as John. Together, they joined the university English club, a meeting place for campus writers, where they befriended two talented and respected faculty members, Margery Bailey and Edith Mirrielees. Bailey saw through John's tough-guy posture and recognized him as the best essayist in her composition class. And Mirrielees, a short story writer, taught John that good writing required discipline. They encouraged him to develop his talent, and he pestered them to listen as he read his stories out loud. By the end of his Stanford career, he had won the faculty's best essay prize and published two stories and a poem in the campus journal, the *Stanford Spectator.* One story, "Fingers of Cloud," explored bindlestiff life and predicted the direction of his later work. But most of what he wrote during this period mocked college life. He had found his writerly discipline but had not yet found his voice.

Even at this early stage in his career, John had unique literary tastes. "This bullheaded independence of his amazed the rest of us," Dook remembered. "He read whatever pleased him."[8] He liked tales of adventure and heroism most of all. In the late twenties and early thirties, when writers such as Gertrude Stein and Ernest Hemingway were introducing new literary styles, Steinbeck preferred the novels of Brian Oswald Donn-Byrne and James Branch Cabell, who wrote in deliberately old-fashioned, poetic prose that reminded John of the Arthurian legends he loved best. He also appreciated Rafael Sabatini's popular pirate tale, *Captain Blood.* Sometime in 1922, under these obscure influences, John began writing a story about Henry Morgan, the seventeenth-century buccaneer who prowled the Caribbean Sea. He would eventually develop the story into his first full-length novel, *Cup of Gold.*

During the summer of 1923, John and his sister Mary enrolled in a marine biology course at a research facility near Pacific Grove. John enjoyed scientific work; with his developing talent for observation and his limitless curiosity, he could have become a capable biologist. But he refused to abandon his first love, literature. He returned to Stanford for the winter and spring of 1924, locked himself in his dorm room, hunched over his notebooks, and revised his story of Henry Morgan.

When the semester ended, he and Dook moved into the Steinbeck summer cottage at Pacific Grove. For a short time, they worked twelve-hour shifts inside the Spreckles factory, where the temperature frequently climbed over one hundred degrees. Disgusted by the conditions, John deliberately picked a fight with a coworker during a lunch break and, just as he planned, was fired. He and Dook then set out for San Francisco where they spent their savings on cheap liquor in the illegal speakeasy bars that continued to sell alcohol during Prohibition. Penniless, they crawled to Long Beach, south of Los Angeles, where they accepted any kind of work they could find: they tried to write mystery novels, they failed as door-to-door salesmen, they even stuffed envelopes to earn money for their trip back to Salinas.

Steinbeck enrolled for one final semester at Stanford in 1925. As with his other forays into academic life, he accomplished little during this last stand. He did continue to work on his writing, however. At the English club, he met Elizabeth Anderson, a published writer who called herself John Breck. Like Edith Mirrielees and Margery Bailey, Breck recognized something special in

Steinbeck. She invited him to the small gatherings of writers she held in her studio. She also let him live in a room attached to her stable, a lean-to without plumbing, electricity, or heat. Luckily, the only material comforts John required during this period were his Corona typewriter, paper, and an endless supply of pencils. By the end of the 1925 school year, he had made a decision: he was going to devote his life to writing, no matter what the consequences of that decision would be. He left Palo Alto for good, never to receive a college degree.

CHAPTER TWO

DETERMINATION

Somewhere in the world there is defeat for everyone. Some are destroyed by defeat, and some made small and mean by victory. Greatness lives in one who triumphs equally over defeat and victory.

—*from* The Acts of King Arthur and His Noble Knights[1]

IN THE LATE TWENTIES, many of the American writers who came of age during World War I—the Lost Generation that included Ernest Hemingway and F. Scott Fitzgerald—settled in Paris. Their breakthrough year was 1925: Hemingway published *In Our Time;* Fitzgerald released *The Great Gatsby.*[2] But John Steinbeck would always follow a different path from his peers, and during the summer of 1925 he lived as far from Paris as he possibly could. He worked as a handyman and chauffeur at Fallen Leaf Lake, a resort lodge near

Lake Tahoe in the High Sierra, and slept in a tent beside the lodge house.

When the camp closed for winter, he obtained a berth on a freighter bound for New York. Steinbeck sailed through the Panama Canal and the Caribbean Sea, retracing the path followed by his grandmother Liza Hamilton on her way to California seventy-five years earlier. After a brief stopover in Cuba, he continued on to Manhattan. As he later recalled, he had never seen anything like the giant metropolis: "There was something monstrous about it—the tall buildings looming to the sky and the lights shining through the falling snow. I crept ashore—frightened and cold and with a touch of panic in my stomach."[3]

John's sister Beth, now married, lived in an apartment in Brooklyn and supported him while he looked for a job. Eventually hired by a construction company, he helped build the first Madison Square Garden on Eighth Avenue and Fiftieth Street, but had little time for his writing. One day, tired and dispirited, he left the job site and never returned. Instead, he enlisted the help of his uncle, Joe Hamilton, who found him a job as a cub reporter for the New York *American*. Steinbeck did not have the self-confidence to be a city journalist, and he still wrote in the flowery style of James Branch Cabell and Brian Oswald Donn-Byrne, hardly appropriate models for hard journalism. So the *American* editors reassigned him to the city courtrooms in the false hope that he would learn from the grizzled veterans of the crime beat.

On his meager reporter's salary, he rented a single room apartment in the Gramercy Park section of Manhattan. Mahlon Blaine, an artist John met during his voyage to New York, lived on the first floor of the apartment building, as did Ted Miller, an old friend from Stanford. With Blaine and Miller, John explored the New York nightlife. He even found a girlfriend, a beautiful showgirl who earned considerably more money than he did and helped support him for several weeks. But, to Miller and Blaine's surprise, John broke off his relationship and, two days later, lost his job at the *American*. He found consolation in his writing, revising his novel about the pirate Henry Morgan, and composing a series of love stories as well.

His devotion to fiction seemed to be paying off in the spring of 1926. He submitted his love stories to Robert M. McBride & Company, a publishing firm interested in young writers. After reading the stories, McBride editor Guy Holt encouraged John to send six more as soon as he could. Completely broke, depending on Ted Miller's generosity and a diet of sardines and crackers, he wrote to survive. But by the time he finished his new stories, Guy Holt had already left McBride for a different publisher, and Holt's editors rejected his work. After hearing the news, John lost his temper and had to be dragged from the McBride offices, kicking and screaming. The next day, he contacted Holt, now at the John Day Company, but Holt's new employers refused to print a short story collection by an unknown writer.

Having exhausted his options in Manhattan, John returned to California, earning his passage as a ship's mate on a freighter bound for San Francisco. The ship's crew appreciated his writing talents, particularly when he helped them compose love letters to girlfriends. But his parents were less appreciative when he returned to Salinas in June. In their eyes, he had achieved nothing during his six months on the East Coast. For that matter, he had achieved almost nothing since his senior year in high school. After a month at Central Avenue, and several discussions about his future, John left home again. First he moved in with Dook Sheffield and his wife in their small apartment in Palo Alto, then he returned to Lake Tahoe.

He worked at Fallen Leaf Lake as a maintenance man until the end of the 1926 vacation season. Then, determined to finish his first novel, he stayed in the Tahoe area through the winter as a caretaker on a large estate owned by Alice Brigham, the widow of a San Francisco surgeon. John amused himself in the family's well-stocked library but his nearest neighbor lived almost two miles away. Twice a week, he journeyed on snowshoes to Camp Richardson, a meeting place for the caretakers from the surrounding resorts. There he picked up his mail and tried to fight off the loneliness of his new lifestyle. But he did not complain. He considered this new isolation a necessary preparation for life and literature. "Do you know, one of the things that made me come here was, as you guessed, that I am frightfully afraid of being alone," he wrote to a friend during that long winter. "The fear of the dark is only part of it. I wanted to break that fear in the middle, because I am afraid much of my existence is going to be more or less alone, and I might as well go into training for it."[4]

He finally found a companion in February 1927 when Lloyd Shebley, a government agent with the Department of Fish and Game, arrived at Camp Richardson on his way to a nearby fish hatchery. John helped the newcomer carry his bags across the snow-covered landscape. Coming to a wire fence in their path, John pulled a revolver out of his coat and tried to shoot the wires down. "He scared the devil out of me," Shebley said later. "It was a while before I even felt safe in the man's company."[5] But the two men needed each other. John helped Shebley at the hatchery, and Shebley helped John chop firewood. John also hired some area bindlestiffs to help with the logging and, as always, paid them a quarter each for telling him their life stories.

That March a new magazine, the *Smoker's Companion*, accepted John's fairy tale, "The Gifts of Iban." The story of a sprite who tries to win the love of a fairy by giving her gifts of sunlight and moonlight, "The Gifts of Iban" displayed John's continuing fascination with ancient myths and legends. But he knew that most editors and critics undervalued fantasy writing, and he published the story under a pseudonym, John Stern. He accepted the *Smoker's Companion's* payment of seven dollars and told few people about his first published story.

Steinbeck stayed at the Brigham estate through the following winter and found the isolation easier to accept as he worked deeper into his novel about Henry Morgan. Adopting a technique he would use throughout his life, he listened to classical music as he wrote to improve the rhythm of his words. He knew that the Morgan novel, which he now called "Cup of Gold," would not be his best work, but he hoped it would advance his career. "Isn't it a shame . . . that a thing which has as many indubitably fine things in it as my Cup of Gold, should be, as a whole, utterly worthless?" he wrote to a friend that winter.[6] Hesitantly, in April 1928, he sent the manuscript to Ted Miller in New York, hoping Miller would be able to find a publisher.

That same month, he left the Brigham estate to work with Lloyd Shebley at the fish hatchery, raising trout for California's rivers. In addition to the light work of the hatchery, John conducted tours of the premises. He described the features of the hatchery in made-up scientific language and loved when the tourists called him "Doctor." During one of these tours, in June, he met two sisters from San Francisco, Carol and Idell Henning. He liked Carol immediately and took her out several times before she returned to San Francisco in July. Considering John's strange behavior during this period—he often drank too much, hoping to fight off his loneliness—their dates were relatively successful. Carol appreciated John's sense of humor, and he felt comfortable in her company. So even after the Department of Fish and Game fired him for wrecking the hatchery's new truck, he felt that he had finally made some progress in his life: now he had a girlfriend and a completed novel.

He followed Carol to San Francisco in the fall, found a day job at a warehouse, and worked on his stories at night. Carol took an active interest in politics and social causes during this period, introducing John to new philosophies and critics of American society, including members of Communist organizations. Unlike Carol, John disliked the Communists. He sympathized with the plight of the poor, and particularly with the bindlestiffs, but the Communists' proposals—to overthrow the American political system and redistribute money and wealth to all U.S. citizens—seemed too radical for him. In fact, he would never abandon his basic faith in the U.S. government, not even in the years when he became one of the most vocal critics of government policy.

Besides, John was too concerned about his own financial straits in the late twenties to worry about broader social issues. He quit his warehouse job in December to devote all of his time to writing. He survived this difficult period only because his father supported him, sending him $25 each month and allowing him to live at the Pacific Grove cottage. Bolstered by his father's money and faith, Steinbeck settled into a daily pattern. In the mornings, he worked on "The Green Lady," a new story he agreed to revise for his friend Toby Street. Then, when he finished his day's work, he wandered the town of Monterey, observing the canneries, the sardine boats, and all of the people who made the town unique.

Early in 1929, he received news from Ted Miller: Robert M. McBride & Company, the publishers who rejected his New York stories, agreed to publish *Cup of Gold.* McBride paid John a $250 advance against future sales and hired Mahlon Blaine to illustrate the book's cover. The McBride editors hoped that Blaine's good reputation would help sell John's book. Blaine's cartoon, depicting a trio of somber pirates holding an ornate gold cup, actually did help sales, but only by accident. Seeing the colorful dust jacket, most bookstore clerks stocked Steinbeck's first novel in the juvenile section, and parents bought the book as a Christmas present for their young sons.[7] John hated the Blaine cover but would not complain too loudly: *Cup of Gold* sold more copies than his next two books put together.

Cup of Gold is the story of a Welsh country boy, Henry Morgan, who leaves his home to become a feared pirate only to find that power and respect cannot bring him happiness. Full of dashing heroes and evil villains, magic and sorcerers, the novel revisits the myths and legends that inspired John as a child. In fact, it recalls so many of the stories John treasured that it often loses focus. Still, it offers an interesting view of John's concerns during these early years. Henry, like young John, wants to escape his parents' influence. Also like John, Henry craves adventure and glory. And, as would later happen to Steinbeck, success separates Morgan from his friends and family. Although it failed financially as well as artistically—Carol called it blarney[8]—*Cup of Gold* was a valuable learning experience for John and an important first attempt at literary greatness.

Steinbeck took a part-time job as a department store clerk during the summer of 1929 and shared an apartment with Carl Wilhelmson, an old friend from the Stanford English club. In time, Wilhelmson would publish a novel, *Midsummernight,* and a children's book. But in 1929 Carl, like John, struggled with his writing. "Like a squad of fleas, ferocious and very serious," John wrote in November, "we still make forays and dignified campaigns against the body of art. It is funny and a little sad (for the onlooker) and lots of fun (for us)."[9] Under Wilhelmson's influence, Steinbeck transformed Toby Street's "The Green Lady" into a completely new novel, which he called "To an Unknown God." He also transformed his personal life. He surprised Carol with a proposal in November. "Marry me," he told her, "and you will be swathed in furs, have your own swimming pool, and your name in lights."[10] Carol's family never trusted John, whose future seemed so uncertain, and discouraged the engagement. But Olive and John Ernst Steinbeck were thrilled to see their son settling down. John and Carol were married on January 14, 1930 at a courthouse in Glendale, California.

1930 would be one of John's busiest years as a writer. He produced a wide variety of stories and wrote a great many pages—most of which he never published—while experimenting with modern writing techniques. During the previous year, he had read Ernest Hemingway's short story "The Killers" and had told Carol that Hemingway was "the finest writer alive."[11] Hemingway's sharp, unadorned sentences suggested an alternative to the flowery poetics of John's old style. (John continued to admire Hemingway's work, even after Hemingway treated him rudely during their first and only meeting in 1944.) He also discovered the work of John

Carol Steinbeck (in dark cap) and John (behind her) enjoyed sailing during their years together.

Dos Passos, whose pastiche technique of combining fiction with newspaper clippings and other elements of mass media suggested new ways to represent the world in its entirety. Struggling with these new influences, John began a cycle of experimental short stories called "Dissonant Symphony." Unfortunately he never mastered the experiments to his satisfaction, could not find a publisher, and destroyed the manuscript. Hemingway's lean style would appear in some of his later works, as would Dos Passos's pastiche, but Steinbeck would never feel comfortable with ideas or techniques he did not discover himself.

He finished "To an Unknown God" in April and sent it to Ted Miller. To John's disappointment, McBride & Company requested a rewrite. Although his father increased his allowance to $50 per month after his wedding, he now needed money desperately. He set aside all of his serious writing projects and churned out a 63,000-word pulp fiction mystery called "Murder at Full Moon," hoping that Ted Miller could once again sell an inferior manuscript. "It is quite obvious that people do not want to buy the things I have been writing," John admitted to Miller. "Therefore, to make the money I need, I must write the things they want to read. . . . Remember that when this manuscript makes you sick. And remember that it makes me a great deal sicker than it does you."[12] Few people liked the novel any more than John did.

In the fall of 1930, in an attempt to jumpstart his career, John hired a new literary agency, McIntosh & Otis, to take on the work Ted Miller had been doing free of charge. The founders of the firm, Mavis McIntosh and Elizabeth Otis, had earned the respect of the New York literary establishment after only three years of partnership. In time, Mavis and Elizabeth would become more than John's business associates; they would become sensitive editors, valued friends, and the first line of protection between John and the press. While Mavis rejected "To an Unknown God" in 1930, she loved Steinbeck's idea for a new cycle of connected short stories. Biding his time until Mavis could sell one of his manuscripts, John briefly accepted a job with Pacific Biologicals in Monterey.

Pacific Biologicals collected and treated samples of marine life for high school biology classes. Its founder and principal employee, Ed Ricketts, grew up in Chicago, served in the Army Medical Corps during World War I, attended both Illinois State Normal University and the University of Chicago, and, like John, never received a degree. When John met him, Ricketts was living at his laboratory on Monterey's "cannery row," site of the city's sardine and fruit packing plants. To John, Ed Ricketts seemed like a complete man and role model: a scholar and a drinker, a scientist and a romantic. Ed revived John's interest in biology and helped him hone his observation skills. After a morning of writing, John would walk to Ed's laboratory, help him collect starfish or octopi, and discuss his latest brainstorms.

Under Ed's influence, John began to synthesize his ideas about biology, ecology, and social reform into a grand theory about human interaction. He came to believe that people acted differently in large groups, that crowds take on personalities different from the personalities of individuals. He described his theory in a detailed letter to Dook Sheffield: "The fascinating thing to me is the way the group has a soul, a drive . . . which in no way resembles the same things possessed by the men who make up the group. These groups have always been considered as individuals multiplied. And they are not so. They are beings in themselves, entities."[13] John called the new group entity a phalanx, from the Greek word for spider. In years to come, he would adapt his phalanx theory to his changing concerns and perspectives, and give it a central place in his personal philosophy.

In December 1931, John shipped a collection of short stories, *The Pastures of Heaven,* to Mavis McIntosh. Although Mavis had reservations about the finished product, she succeeded in contracting a publisher, Cape and Smith. Robert O. Ballou, the book's editor, even offered to sign John to a three-book contract. John received the news on February 27, 1932, his thirtieth birthday. After so many false starts, he believed that *The Pastures of Heaven* would be his big break. But Cape and Smith declared bankruptcy a month later. Ballou took the manuscript with him to his next company, Brewer, Warren and Putnam, but the company did not have enough money to publicize or market the book, and John saw his dream of literary success fade again. When *The Pastures of Heaven* finally appeared in October 1933, the American economy had sunk to its lowest point in the Great Depression and few people were willing to spend money on the work of an unknown writer. The book received a handful of strong reviews, including one in *The Nation* predicting that if Steinbeck "could add social insight to his present equipment he would be a first-rate novelist."[14] But Brewer, Warren and Putnam failed to sell even a thousand copies. And soon it too declared bankruptcy.

Steinbeck developed the idea for *The Pastures of Heaven*—a volume of connected short stories—after listening to the reminiscences of a friend who had grown up in an isolated California community. In his stories, Steinbeck called the community Las Pasturas del Cielo (The Pastures of Heaven) and introduced a well-intentioned family, the Monroes, as its most important residents. Despite their basic kindness, the Monroes wreak havoc on their neighbors' lives, inspiring greed in some people, lust in others. In an economical style derived from Hemingway, Steinbeck describes a separate disaster in each story. By the final story, when a stranger looking down at the pastures announces, "I always like to look down there and think how quiet and easy a man could live on a little place,"[15] the book emerges as a parable about the difference between appearance and reality in American society.

As *The Pastures of Heaven* traveled its tortuous course through the New York publishing community, John tried desperately to revive "To an Unknown God." Another new acquaintance, Joseph Campbell, influenced the final shape of that book. A college professor and the future author of *The Masks of God*, a study of mythology in human history, Campbell became a willing sounding board for John's ideas. He encouraged John to study mythology more closely—particularly fertility myths—and provided the support John needed finally to master the novel.

John's hard work and determination bore fruit in early 1933. Robert Ballou started his own publishing company and accepted Steinbeck's reworked novel, now called *To a God Unknown*. At the same time Simon & Schuster, the major New York firm, also offered to publish the novel. After years of anonymity, John Steinbeck suddenly found himself in the midst of a bidding war between publishers. Since he appreciated Ballou's friendship and faith in *The Pastures of Heaven,* he signed with Robert O. Ballou and Company, thereby rejecting the stability and clout of the big firm and perhaps delaying his material comfort a little longer. Still, at thirty-one years of age, John was the author of a published novel and a collection of short stories, an influential literary agency represented him in New York, and he had another novel in production. He was finally poised for success as a fiction writer, and poised to fulfill his parents' expectations.

Then, in March, Olive Steinbeck suffered a massive stroke and her son's life took yet another strange turn.

CHAPTER THREE

STEINBECK COUNTRY

Noble they may be, sir, but famished they are. They arrive in swarms like locusts and strip the king's larders bare. A defeated knight is, if anything, hungrier than a victor.

—*from* The Acts of King Arthur and His Noble Knights[1]

OLIVE'S STROKE PARALYZED the left side of her body. She required almost constant attention. John's sisters had their own families to care for, and John Ernst was too devastated by his wife's sickness to be of much help. So John, the spoiled son, took over as head of the family and chief nurse. His new responsibilities helped him focus his energies; he wrote to escape his sadness. In a letter written that summer, Steinbeck acknowledged that his experiences were changing him: "I grow less complicated all the time and that is a joy to me. The forces that used to tug in various directions have all started to pull in me. I have a book to write. I think about it for a while and then I write it. There is nothing more."[2] First he completed a novella inspired by his own childhood, "The Red Pony." Then he compiled notes about Monterey and planned a new novel set in the community surrounding the canneries. Between shifts at his mother's bedside, he completed three-quarters of the book he would call *Tortilla Flat.*

Robert O. Ballou and Company finally published *To a God Unknown* in late November. Of the 1,498 copies printed, the company sold only 598. Adding to his earnings from *Cup of Gold, Pastures of Heaven,* and the few short stories he had published, Steinbeck now had made only $870 in seven years of professional writing.

To a God Unknown traces the western migration of Joseph Wayne, who arrives in the Salinas Valley after crossing the continent (like John Adolph Grosssteinbeck) and develops an intimate, almost religious, bond with his new land. By the end of the novel, this bond grows so strong that Wayne takes his own life, believing his sacrifice will end a long drought. In its dense imagery, stilted language, and mystical plot line—inspired by Steinbeck's conversations with Joseph Campbell—*To a God Unknown* displays Steinbeck's penchant for experimentation. But its focus on the region surrounding the Salinas Valley—which would soon be known as Steinbeck Country—suggests that he also was finding his voice and true subject matter.

Although *To a God Unknown* failed commercially, it greatly advanced Steinbeck's career. McIntosh and Otis were able to convince magazine editors that Steinbeck, now the author of three published books, was an important new talent. During the Depression, when literary magazines were more affordable and more popular than books, writers depended on the magazines for their survival. So Steinbeck celebrated when the *North American Review* bought five of his newest stories. He earned $90 for the first two sections of "The Red Pony" and comparable fees for "The Murder," "The Raid," and "The White Quail."

At the same time, Carol found a part-time job with the Emergency Relief Organization, a government agency assisting the nation's poorest areas, particularly those areas affected by the intensifying agricultural crisis of the mid- and late thirties. Severe drought, decades of poor land management, and the spread of mechanized farming techniques drove tenant farmers from their lands in the Midwest and Southwest. Evicted farmers, known as Okies or Dust Bowl refugees, flooded the state of California looking for work. There the refugees clashed with black, Mexican, and Filipino migrants who normally harvested the region. In addition, labor organizers and members of the Communist Party spearheaded worker strikes and created unions to fight for better wages.

As Carol assisted Mexican migrants near Monterey, John investigated the crisis on his own. He met with union leaders and Dust Bowl refugees who organized a local cotton strike. Their stories haunted John for weeks. As one friend remembers, in early 1934 Steinbeck began to think seriously about politics and the nation's economic collapse: "He thought the country was coming apart, and that if something wasn't done fast a revolution would break out."[3] Steinbeck hoped to avoid revolution. He supported the policies of President Franklin Delano

This Okie home, located near Marysville, California, was typical of the living conditions the destitute Okies endured during the thirties.

Roosevelt, whose New Deal program included large-scale relief for the needy. As he researched the farming crisis, however, he believed it was his duty as a writer to point out the strengths and weaknesses of everyone involved: the farm owners, the workers, the Communist organizers, and even the government.

He briefly set aside these new concerns when his mother died, on February 19, 1934. As he mourned, he worried about his father. John Ernst had been getting weaker since a bout of illness in October and could no longer be left alone. John and Carol took him to Pacific Grove in March, where they watched over him for a short time. But John Ernst realized that he was becoming a burden to his son and daughter-in-law and moved back to Salinas.

After his father's departure, John finished the *Tortilla Flat* manuscript. To his surprise, Robert Ballou refused to publish the novel, suggesting it was "too slight," and not serious enough to attract an audience.[4] So even though "The Murder"—one of the stories published in the *North American Review*—won the 1934 O. Henry Award as the year's best short story, and even though he had been writing well and continuously for the past year, Steinbeck's career seemed on the verge of a major collapse once again.

Then he got lucky; unbeknownst to Steinbeck, men in a different part of the country were determining his future. Ben Abramson, a Chicago bookstore owner who had been watching Steinbeck's career for some time, passed a copy of *The Pastures of Heaven* to his friend Pascal "Pat" Covici, a part owner of a failing New York publishing firm Covici-Friede. Covici also admired Steinbeck's talent and immediately called McIntosh and Otis to inquire about the writer's future work. Since Ballou had already rejected *Tortilla Flat,* Covici offered to publish the novel and reprint Steinbeck's three other titles. Grateful that anyone had taken an interest in his work, Steinbeck signed a contract with Covici. He would stay with Pat for the rest of his writing career.

Late in the summer of 1934, Steinbeck began a book about the California farm labor crisis. Originally intending to write a nonfiction account of a union organizer's life, he decided to write a novel to protect the union men who lived under a constant threat of violence. Earlier in the summer, San Francisco police raided a longshoreman strike on the city docks, beating dockworkers in an attempt to scare them back to work. That event, remembered as Bloody Thursday, was only the latest example of anti-labor violence erupting all over the country. Sometimes the police were involved; more often, civilian vigilantes, fearing a disruption to their business, attacked striking workers. Against this backdrop, Steinbeck set to work on his fourth novel, *In Dubious Battle.*

The novel follows the life of Jim Nolan, an inarticulate ex-convict who joins the Communist Party and leads an apple-pickers' strike. Nolan supports the Communist Party because it seems to be doing good work for people who need help. "In jail there were some Party men," he remembers. "They talked to me. Everything's been a mess, all my life. Their lives weren't messes. They were working toward something. I want to work toward something. I feel dead. I thought I might get alive again."[5] But Nolan slowly changes over the course of the novel, from a young man looking to "get alive again" to a ruthless leader who risks the lives of others for the sake of his cause. He is the first in a long line of Steinbeck characters to test the phalanx idea; he brings good men together and creates a violent mob.

Steinbeck finished the long novel in just five months. Fast-paced, action-packed, it displayed a mature literary voice and style. But it drew harsh criticism, as Steinbeck had predicted. Strike organizers objected to the book's unflattering depictions of union men. California farmers objected to the portrayal of vigilante violence and an unresponsive police force. Many accused him of racism, since all the characters in the novel are white while a large percentage of the actual California migrants were black, Mexican, and Filipino. But the most common criticisms came from businessmen who claimed that Steinbeck was a Communist, and from Communists who claimed that he was not enough of a Communist.

As Steinbeck finished *In Dubious Battle,* his father weakened and became less alert. He died in early May. For Steinbeck, John Ernst's death was even more heartbreaking than his mother's. "I feel very badly, not about his death, but about his life," he wrote to a friend in late May, "for he told me only a few months ago that he had never done anything he wanted to do."[6] Steinbeck resolved to pursue his own dream relentlessly in order to avoid his father's fate. It was therefore fitting that *Tortilla Flat* appeared in bookstores five days after his father's death.

Tortilla Flat is a story about *paisanos*, Mexican and Italian residents of a poor section of Monterey. They work in the canneries only when they need money, and only when they cannot steal what they need; they spend the rest of their days adventuring and drinking wine. The novel, written as an adaptation of an Arthurian legend, centers on a band of friends who live together in a beat-up shack owned by their leader, Danny. As Steinbeck writes in the introduction, Danny and his friends are "clean of commercialism, free of the complicated systems of American business, and,

Two of the best-known actors of the time, Hedy Lamarr and John Garfield, starred in the movie version of Tortilla Flat*, released in 1942.*

having nothing that can be stolen, exploited, or mortgaged, that system has not attacked them vigorously."[7] Their adventures are comic, but they also represent veiled critiques of America's obsession with property, status, and money. As in his future novels *Cannery*

Row and *Sweet Thursday*, Steinbeck concludes *Tortilla Flat* with a party, an event that offers the *paisanos* the ultimate freedom from social and economic constraints imposed upon them.

Steinbeck portrays the *paisanos* as men who live a simpler, nobler, freer lifestyle than the members of the white society who condemn them. Yet *Tortilla Flat* also mocks the minority community. Danny and his friends seem too simple and too lazy; they accept their poverty and do not suffer. In his later life and work, Steinbeck would prove sympathetic to the nation's minorities and advocate the expansion of civil rights. Even during his days on the Spreckles ranches, his sympathies lay with his bindlestiff coworkers, not with men like his father who controlled the government and economy. But in his fiction, particularly his early work, these ethnically and racially different men and women usually appear only in comic relief—a common flaw among white writers of the age and an unfortunate flaw in Steinbeck's personal vision.

Most major newspapers published strong reviews of *Tortilla Flat* and the book sold well, appealing to a Depression audience hungering for a funny story to make them forget their own economic problems. Despite Steinbeck's distaste for publicity—he refused to submit a photograph of himself for the book's cover—he agreed to sit for several interviews. The first feature article about him, in the June 2, 1935 issue of the *San Francisco Chronicle*, focused on his weathered appearance, his strong physique, and his attachment to the California landscape, and set the tone for later publicity:

> *Down out of the hills he came, he said; he felt as if he had somehow always lived in them. And John Steinbeck looks as if he might have; of giant height, sunburned, with fair hair and fair mustache and eyes the blue of the Pacific on a sunny day, and a deep, quiet, slow voice. He belongs to this Coast, the Monterey Bay, the ranges and cliffs of Big Sur country.*[8]

The struggling writer quickly became a celebrity. By mid-August, he had earned $300 in royalties on the novel and $4,000 for the movie rights, purchased by Paramount Studios. (Paramount failed to make the movie; MGM produced an uninspired film adaptation in 1942.) In December, he learned that *Tortilla Flat* had won the 1935 Best Novel prize from the Commonwealth Club of California. He recognized a certain irony in the fact that *Tortilla Flat,* a book he had written for his own amusement and to take his mind off of his mother's illness, should be the first novel to succeed. "Curious that this second-rate book, written for relaxation, should cause this fuss," he wrote to Elizabeth Otis. "People are actually taking it seriously."[9]

In September 1935, John and Carol drove to Mexico City in an attempt to escape the numerous requests for interviews, books, articles, and speeches that followed the publication of *Tortilla Flat.* They spent three months there, relaxing after three years of economic and emotional hardship. When they returned to California, they began searching for a new place to live, away from the distractions John now faced. In April 1936, they built a house on two acres in Los Gatos canyon, 50 miles north of Monterey. The new house had no telephone and no electricity, so when John built an 8-foot fence around the property, the Steinbecks were almost entirely secluded.

At Los Gatos, John began a new story based on his experiences with the bindlestiffs. It began as a children's book, but now he could not decide on the right format. He resolved his dilemma by imagining his ideal audience: the California workers, the same migrants he was writing about. He knew these men were not reading novels. But he also knew they attended plays performed by traveling theater groups. Since Steinbeck had never written a play before, he decided to do the next best thing; he wrote a novel that could easily be adapted to the stage. As a result, *Of Mice and Men,* more than any of his previous works, would depend heavily on dialogue.

In August, as he completed *Of Mice and Men,* he accepted the proposal of a *San Francisco News* editor to write a series of articles about the migrant labor camps appearing all over the California countryside. As the celebrity author of *Tortilla Flat* and the astute observer of *In Dubious Battle,* Steinbeck seemed the perfect choice for the job. He bought an old bakery truck, or "pie wagon," and fitted the rear hold with a cot, an icebox, and some trunks—creating a small room for roadside camping. He toured the San Joaquin Valley with federal agents monitoring the influx of Dust Bowl refugees. He saw once-proud Oklahoma and Texas families living in cardboard boxes and abandoned sewer pipes, fighting with each other and with the black, Mexican, and Filipino workers who competed for the same jobs. He watched long lines of broken-down cars crawling across the Mojave Desert from the east. And he saw how only a small minority of Californians tried to help the 300,000 poor and dispossessed settling by the roadsides.[10] Most importantly, he met Tom Collins, the manager of the Arvin Sanitary Camp, one of fifteen government facilities offering migrants a clean, safe place to live while they searched for jobs. Collins loaned Steinbeck his extensive notes on the lives of the migrants he met. John treasured these notes and referred to them frequently in the coming years.

Steinbeck composed his articles in the cabin of the pie wagon when he was not out working with the migrants. In September, he published a seven-part series in the *San Francisco News* titled, "The Harvest Gypsies"—with photographs by Dorothea Lange—depicting the meager living conditions inside Okie camps. He also published a feature story in *Nation* magazine titled, "Dubious Battle in California." In these articles, he predicted that desperate Okies would improve their living conditions with or without government or farm-owner support. Steinbeck suggested that the government should relieve the starving migrants and act as mediator between the laborers and the wealthy farm owners. Such proposals were dangerous in 1936. Farm owners accused Steinbeck of being a Communist and a public menace. They backed their accusations with the threat of vigilante violence, but Steinbeck refused to be intimidated.

As Steinbeck traveled between Los Gatos and the San Joaquin Valley in late 1936 and early 1937, Covici-Friede prepared *Of Mice and Men* for publication. After the success of *Tortilla Flat,* the company had no problem convincing retailers to order copies of a new novel by John Steinbeck. The Book-of-the-Month Club chose the novel as its main selection in January, guaranteeing the sale of over 100,000 copies even before the book was officially released.

Of Mice and Men recounts an episode in the lives of two bindlestiffs, George and Lennie, who roam the California countryside looking for work. Lennie, a large, mentally handicapped man, depends on George for his survival in a hostile world; George is resourceful and smart, but his loyalty to the accident-prone Lennie prevents him from realizing his dreams. Nevertheless, George continues to scheme and plan for his future, and he inspires

A still photo from the pivotal scene of Of Mice and Men, *which starred Lon Chaney Jr. as Lennie (left) and Burgess Meredith as George*

those around him to dream as well. "Maybe we'd have a cow or a goat," George says, describing his plans to buy a small farm. "We could live offa the fatta the lan'," replies a wide-eyed Lennie.[11] Sadly, the two men never come any closer to their dream. George is continually forced to choose between his own success and his friendship with Lennie. And Lennie's inability to understand the world leads to his own death and to the death of the dream he shared with George.

While some critics dismissed the novel as an insignificant fairy tale, or criticized Steinbeck for his interest in violence, *Of Mice and Men* made all the bestseller lists. Steinbeck was forced to travel into town almost daily to conduct business and to sit for interviews. He discouraged outsiders from seeking too much information about his private life, arriving at one press conference carrying a bottle of brandy and growling at the reporters, "All right, bring 'em on."[12] But he became famous in spite of himself. As planned, he developed a stage version of the novel for the Theater Union, a San Francisco troupe performing for the city's striking dock workers. After sixteen performances, he revised the script again as his theatrical agent, Anne Laurie Williams, negotiated an even bigger production on New York's Broadway, with George S. Kaufman as director.

As his career boomed, however, his relationship with Carol was falling apart. Since their brief Mexico vacation almost two years earlier, their lives had taken extreme turns. John was now a famous writer and a social activist and Carol was not sure where she fit in his life. Realizing that something had to be done to save their marriage, the Steinbecks decided to take another vacation. First they spent almost three weeks in Manhattan with Pat Covici, meeting with the press and introducing themselves to the national media. Frequently drunk—usually to compensate for his shyness and distaste for media attention—John was ill-tempered and mean. But Carol also drank too much. She disappeared in the city for long periods of time and embarrassed Steinbeck publicly. In late May, when they finally boarded the S.S. *Drottningholm* for Sweden, they were both relieved to leave the scene of so much distress. Only the horrible living conditions on board the *Drottningholm* brought them together again. Stowed in a dark, windowless room in the hull of the ship, the Steinbecks found comfort in each other for the first time in months. After visiting most of the major cities of northern Europe, they returned to California in the fall of 1937.

Steinbeck signed a contract for the Broadway production of *Of Mice and Men* shortly after his return. A success in the theater would broaden Steinbeck's audience and pay handsomely, so Steinbeck wanted the play to succeed. But he did not want to devote his time to the numerous rewrites demanded by director Kaufman. In November, Kaufman invited Steinbeck to a house in Bucks County, Pennsylvania, where he stayed until he finished the script to Kaufman's satisfaction. Desperate to get back to California, he incorporated some of the changes the director asked for, and then refused to do any more. "My work is done here," he said to his backers. "I wish you gentlemen luck."[13] The show opened at the Music Box Theatre on November 23, 1937, an important event in the life of any young writer. But Steinbeck kept his word: his work was done, and he did not attend the opening night or any other Broadway performance of *Of Mice and Men.* Despite Steinbeck's lack of interest, the show was a hit. In the *New Republic*, reviewer Stanley Young enthused, "I have never seen a play quite like it, have no previous acquaintance with the nature of its suspenses, or with the curious artistic satisfaction that its development affords."[14] After a run of 207 performances, the New York Drama Critics Circle voted *Of Mice and Men* the best play of the 1938 season, over Thornton Wilder's equally influential classic, *Our Town.*

The show's success contributed to Steinbeck's runaway fame. Almost everywhere he turned he found someone who expected something of him—his time, his work, his money. Hollywood executives begged him for scripts. Impoverished fans asked him for support as they weathered the financial storms of the Depression. Some of his oldest friends grew jealous of his fame. And almost everyone wondered if he would let fame change him. Complicating matters, Pat Covici published a limited edition of *The Red Pony* in 1937. He charged $10 for each specially printed, numbered, and signed book, a large sum during the Depression. Critics rejected *The Red Pony* because of its price rather than for its content. They charged that the writer was turning his back on the poor workers who populated his fiction; they said he was selling out.

In content, at least, *The Red Pony* does not support those charges. It follows the life of a young boy, Jody, who grows up on a California ranch and cares for Gabilan, his pony colt (just as John had cared for Jill, his own red pony). Simply—often beautifully—written, it is one of Steinbeck's most autobiographical stories, a parable about the difference between childhood and adulthood in the modern world.

In the winter of 1937–38, with government approval, Steinbeck revisited migrant camps all over California, usually with photographer Horace Bristol or Tom Collins, the manager of the Arvin camp, in tow. Bristol shot more than two thousand pictures while Steinbeck spoke to the migrants, helped them fight the effects of a devastating flood, and used his pie wagon to transport food and supplies to the destitute. What he saw disturbed him terribly, and he scrambled to find a way to improve the migrants' lives. He and Bristol accepted an offer from *Life* magazine to report on the crisis in return for expense money and contributions to relief organizations. *Life* rejected his articles, however, because they advocated changes that still seemed too radical to the anticommunist forces in the nation.

Abandoned by newspapers and magazines, Steinbeck searched for a new way to attack the atrocious conditions in central California. First he donated his old *San Francisco News* articles to the Simon J. Lubin Society, a San Francisco philanthropic organization. The organization sold the articles and their accompanying photographs under the title *Their Blood Is Strong* and donated the proceeds to relief agencies around California. Then Steinbeck allowed members of the United Cannery, Agricultural, Packing and Allied Workers of America to create the John Steinbeck Committee for Migrant Relief. Finally, he set to work on a fictional representation of the migrant crisis. After several false starts, including an unfinished novel called "The Oklahomans" and a satirical attack called "L'Affaire Lettuceberg," he mapped out an epic novel that would portray all sides of the conflict between farm owners and migrant workers. The new book was a joint effort: as John wrote, Carol proofread and typed. Work on the manuscript slowed when Carol had her tonsils removed, and nearly ground to a halt when Covici-Friede declared bankruptcy in August 1938. But Pat Covici eventually landed a job with Viking Press, a major New York publishing house, and took Steinbeck with him. Covici-Friede's misfortune became Steinbeck's good fortune. As he finished his masterpiece novel, *The Grapes of Wrath*, he knew he had a large organization behind him, ready to devote its energies to the novel's publication. All the pieces were now in place for Steinbeck's heroic breakthrough.

CHAPTER FOUR

VINTAGE

He looked down on the gray and dusty bread, and perhaps because he had not eaten or rested, his temper flared and he reversed his spear and beat the gate with the butt until it roared with oaken protest.

—*from* The Acts of King Arthur and His Noble Knights[1]

FAN LETTERS POURED IN from all over the country. Reporters begged for interviews. Major public figures such as Charlie Chaplin, the most popular movie star in the world, traveled to Los Gatos to meet the writer of *Tortilla Flat* and *Of Mice and Men.* The traffic around John Steinbeck's house grew so heavy that it interfered with his work, so he and Carol moved to an even more secluded ranch north of Los Gatos. There, Steinbeck labored over a large and growing manuscript.

The California migrant novel became his single obsession. "My life isn't very long," he wrote in a journal he kept during this period, "and I must get *one* good book written before it ends. The others have been makeshifts, experiments, practices. For the first time I am working on a real book that is not limited and that will take every bit of experience and thought and feeling that I have."[2] Writing five or six days a week, sometimes as many as two thousand words at a stretch, Steinbeck worked himself to exhaustion. "John had never been so concentrated," his sister Beth remembered later. "You almost couldn't talk to him."[3]

The new novel absorbed him so completely that he hardly noticed when Viking published his second short story collection, *The Long Valley*, in September 1938. Most of the stories had already appeared in magazines and some, such as *The Red Pony*, had also been sold in limited-edition volumes. But *The Long Valley* quickly became a bestseller, convincing readers and reviewers alike that Steinbeck had entered the ranks of the nation's premier writers.

Some of the twelve stories in *The Long Valley*, such as "Johnny Bear," revisit character types Steinbeck introduced in *The Pastures of Heaven* and *Of Mice and Men*, lonely outcasts who cannot speak for themselves.[4] Others, such as "The Murder," explore failing relationships and themes of lost love and lost heroism. Still others, such as "The Chrysanthemums," challenge the reader to make sense of their characters' secret hopes and dreams. As a whole, the collection displays the full range of Steinbeck's interests and the variety of his technique during his most productive and successful creative period.

As the new year approached, Steinbeck finished his new novel. Carol suggested that he call the book "The Grapes of Wrath," alluding to the opening lines of "The Battle Hymn of the Republic":

> *"Mine eyes have seen the glory of the coming of the Lord / He is tramping out the vintage where the grapes of wrath are stored."*

Steinbeck loved the idea; the lyric linked his California migrants with the political and religious struggles of the American past. He knew he had to defend his patriotism because his honest, occasionally brutal book would offend many people in the California farming community. "This will not be a popular book," he wrote to Elizabeth Otis, warning her not to expect *The Grapes of Wrath* to duplicate the success of *Of Mice and Men.* "And it will be a loss to do anything except to print a small edition and watch and print more if there are more orders."[5] But even as he preached caution, he refused to change the substance of his story and fought every one of his editors' revisions. "I am not writing a satisfactory story," he wrote to Pat Covici during one heated debate. "I've done my damndest to rip a reader's nerves to rags. I don't want him satisfied."[6]

The Grapes of Wrath chronicles the flight of an Oklahoma migrant family, the Joads, from their land in the drought-ridden Dust Bowl to the California fruit farms. Like other Okies, the Joads cross the deserts of the Southwest in the hope of finding work along the Pacific coast. But their expectations are too high; the California farms do not need their labor and the advertisements that attract them to the West exaggerate their opportunities. The police and the California government support the farm owners, not the laborers, and few people are willing to help the Joads and their fellow migrants as their wages continue to plummet, their children starve, and their families collapse. "In the souls of the people," Steinbeck writes, "the grapes of wrath are filling and growing heavy, growing heavy for the vintage."[7]

One of the most vivid characters of the novel, a former preacher named Jim Casey, channels the migrants' anger into a new formulation of Steinbeck's phalanx theory:

> *I figgered about the Holy Sperit and the Jesus road. I figgered, "Why do we hang it on God or Jesus? Maybe," I figgered, "maybe it's all men an' all women we love; maybe that's the Holy Sperit—the human sperit—the whole shebang. Maybe all men got one big soul ever'body's a part of.*[8]

Casey transforms the phalanx idea—once a biological and psychological explanation for group action—into a challenge against the injustices of the California migrant experience and an argument for group solidarity, community, and unconditional love. Inspired by Casey's teachings, Tom Joad dedicates himself to the fight for justice, telling his mother:

> *I'll be ever'where—wherever you look. Wherever they's a fight so hungry people can eat, I'll be there. Wherever they's a cop beatin' up a guy, I'll be there. If Casey knowed, why, I'll be in the way guys yell*

when they're mad an'—I'll be in the way kids laugh when they're hungry an' they know supper's ready. An' when our folks eat the stuff they raise an' live in the houses they build—why, I'll be there.[9]

By the end of the novel, each member of the family displays a willingness to follow Tom's lead, make sacrifices for others, and forge a new community through shared suffering. In Steinbeck's terms, the strength of this new community, based on the "human sperit," is the only hope for change.

In early March 1939, Steinbeck received a bound copy of his novel in the mail, 850 pages of the hardest and best writing he had ever done. The reviews that followed praised *The Grapes of Wrath* as one of the most important novels of the decade, though most reviewers tended to see it as a work of protest rather than art. As a featured selection of most book clubs, it reached the broad audience Steinbeck had been seeking. But the reading public was not ready for the kind of book Steinbeck gave them. Graphic scenes—one depicting a woman's bare breast, another describing a urinating turtle—were new to popular fiction in the Depression years; many people condemned Steinbeck for the vulgarity of his images. Others, in order to protect California planters and American big business, tried to condemn him on other grounds. Oklahoma newspapers denied that Dust Bowl conditions were as bad as Steinbeck claimed. Government officials spread false rumors that the migrants themselves hated Steinbeck's book. Several people threatened his life. And tensions barely subsided when First Lady Eleanor Roosevelt spoke up in his defense in April 1940, announcing, "I have never believed that *The Grapes of Wrath* was exaggerated."[10]

Even as the public debated the truth of Steinbeck's account, Viking published 430,000 copies of the novel in the first year and Hollywood producers engaged in a bidding war over the movie rights. Twentieth Century-Fox won the war, paying $75,000. Reporters now tracked Steinbeck's every move, despite his best efforts to avoid attention. He had dreamed his whole life of writing a big, important book, but now that he had written that book and become famous, he resented the public's scrutiny. "I was recognized in [San Francisco] the other day and it made me sick to my stomach," he wrote to his agents in March 1939. "Unless I can stand in a crowd without any self-consciousness and watch things from an uneditorialized point of view, I'm going to have a hell of a hard time."[11]

He escaped to Chicago in April 1939 to work on a documentary with his friend, Pare Lorentz, head of the U.S. Film Service, a government agency that produced educational movies. At President Roosevelt's request, Lorentz was directing *The Fight for Life*, a film about the hazards of childbirth and the need for comprehensive health coverage. He asked Steinbeck to research the latest birthing techniques at Chicago Maternity Center and Steinbeck accepted, appreciating the time away from the media onslaught.

For Carol, however, there was no escape. She had worked long hours as a typist and editor on *The Grapes of Wrath*. At the same time, she discouraged visitors and created a quiet household while her husband wrote. But she grew restless as the novel neared completion, and wanted more of her husband's attention. To her excitement, just after Christmas 1939, she learned that she was pregnant. Steinbeck had mixed feelings about being a father. Whether he was still too insecure to accept the responsibility of fatherhood or simply scared that an infant would interrupt his writing routine, he discouraged the birth. Against her judgment, Carol agreed to have an abortion. Tragically, her doctors botched the procedure, and she contracted a serious infection. Soon she needed a complete hysterectomy, eliminating her chance to give birth again. For a marriage that was already in trouble, this latest disaster was fatal.

Ashamed and heartbroken, Steinbeck again left Los Gatos after completing his work for Lorentz and signed on to another movie project. The national tour of the play *Of Mice and Men* had been a huge success, prompting several Hollywood producers to inquire about the movie rights. In the end, the rights went to Lewis Milestone, who had directed the classic World War I film *All Quiet on the Western Front.* In early June, Steinbeck rented an apartment in Los Angeles and adapted the stage play for film. He hated the work, but Milestone coaxed a solid screenplay out of him anyway. Filming began in August with Lon Chaney Jr. playing Lennie, and Burgess Meredith playing George.

During that same summer, Twentieth Century-Fox filmed *The Grapes of Wrath.* Director John Ford took over the project, with Henry Fonda in the leading role as Tom Joad. Most observers expected studio executives to dilute Steinbeck's social messages, but after pro-

Twentieth Century-Fox's 1940 production of The Grapes of Wrath *starred young actors who later became famous, including Doris Bowdon (second from left), Henry Fonda (third from left), and John Carradine (far right).*

ducer Darryl F. Zanuck researched the migrant camps, he told Steinbeck, "The conditions are much worse than you reported."[12] To Steinbeck's surprise and delight, Zanuck and the studio wanted to portray the camps as he wrote about them. Zanuck even hired John's friend Tom Collins as technical adviser and filmed part of the movie at Collins's Arvin camp. The result is one of the greatest movies ever made. It won both the National Board of Review and the New York Film Critics best picture awards. John Ford won an Oscar and a New York Film Critics award for best director, and actress Jane Darwell, who played Ma Joad, also won an Oscar.

Steinbeck became a major force in American entertainment in the summer of 1940, but his personal life unraveled. Old friends stayed away now that he was a celebrity; new friends drew him deeper into a more glamorous world. And he fell in love with another woman, a twenty-year-old nightclub performer named Gwyn Conger. Beautiful, seductive, and interested in Steinbeck's books, Gwyn captured Steinbeck's attention and held it throughout the summer. At the end of July, Carol and John traveled to Los Angeles together, trying once again to mend their marriage. But after a long, bitter argument, Carol returned home alone. Depressed, John stayed in his hotel room for two weeks. Then he traveled to Pacific Grove and resumed his daily meetings with his old friend Ed Ricketts.

While John was finishing *The Grapes of Wrath*, Ed had written his own book, *Between Pacific Tides*, a major scientific text on the marine ecology of the Pacific coast. Now, free of distractions, Steinbeck approached Ed's research with renewed interest. He and Ed collaborated on a handbook about the marine life of Monterey Bay—a book they never finished—and then planned a research expedition into the Gulf of California (also known as the Sea of Cortez). John made arrangements all through the winter, buying or building equipment and plotting the course. Finally, he assembled a crew, including Carol as cook, and chartered Captain Tony Berry's *Western Flyer*, a sardine boat big enough to brave the seas but small enough to negotiate small coastal inlets. The trip lasted six weeks and covered 4,000 miles. Ed, the more knowledgeable collector and the only trained scientist on the *Flyer*, kept extensive notes of their findings, while John kept the crew together with his enthusiasm and good humor. "If I was just coming into money like he was," Captain Berry remembered later, "I would have had a big head. But he didn't."[13]

As Steinbeck and Ricketts combed the shores of Central America, a new war raged in Europe. Steinbeck had been watching the progress of World War II for some time. In the fall of 1939, he had written to President Roosevelt suggesting an impractical scheme for crippling the economy of Nazi Germany. Now, in June 1940, home from his travels in Mexico, he again wrote to the president offering his observations about the impact of Nazi propaganda in Central America. "It is probable that you have considered this situation in all its facets," Steinbeck wrote. "However, if my observation can be of any use to you, I shall be very glad to speak with you for I am sure that this problem is one of the most important faced by the nation."[14] Roosevelt called Steinbeck to Washington for a twenty-minute meeting, where the two men forged a friendship that would prove mutually beneficial in the years to come.

That summer, Steinbeck visited the Mexican village of Pátzcuaro to work on a documentary about local sanitation practices, a small project suggested to him by director Herbert Kline. The Pátzcuaro water supply was poisoned, but traditional healers and shamans encouraged villagers to drink from it anyway. After extensive research, Steinbeck wrote *The Forgotten Village*, a screenplay that dramatized the conflict between local traditions and modern technology. *The Forgotten Village* appeared in theaters in 1941 and received positive reviews, including another endorsement from Eleanor Roosevelt, but it made little impression on a U.S. public preparing to enter World War II. For Steinbeck, the film was merely a constructive way to exercise his talents during one of the least productive periods of his writing career.

Steinbeck returned to Los Gatos when filming began in late 1940. Slipping into another deep depression over his failing marriage, he began to drink heavily. One night he heard Gwyn Conger's voice on the radio; she was performing at a San Francisco studio. Without telling Carol where he was going, he drove to the city to meet Gwyn, beginning a routine of deception he would continue for weeks. Finally, in early 1941, Steinbeck told Carol about his love for Gwyn. Surprisingly, Carol did not give up on the marriage. In a May 1941 letter to Mavis McIntosh, John suggested that he and Carol would stay together: "My nerves cracked to pieces and I told Carol the whole thing, told her how deeply involved I was [with Gwyn] and how little was left. She said she wanted what was left and was going to fight. So there we are. All in the open, all above board. I'm staying with Carol as I must."[15] The Steinbecks sold the house at Los Gatos, the site of so much unhappiness, and moved to Monterey. But by the end of May, Carol realized their situation was hopeless and moved out. She had encouraged and supported

Steinbeck while he searched for his literary voice. She protected him from worldly interruptions so that he could produce some of the most important fiction of the 1930s. She guided the production of *The Grapes of Wrath*, which won the 1940 Pulitzer Prize. But now she was finally giving up and would never marry again.

On his own for the first time in more than a decade, Steinbeck foundered. He helped his friend Lewis Milestone prepare a movie adaptation of *The Red Pony*. He also oversaw the publication of *Sea of Cortez: A Leisurely Journal of Travel and Research*, the account of the *Western Flyer* expedition, co-authored by Ed Ricketts. Then, in October, at President Roosevelt's request, Steinbeck volunteered with the Foreign Information Service (FIS), the agency leading the fight against Nazi wartime propaganda. He interviewed refugees from war-torn Europe and wrote government radio broadcasts. In this modest way, Steinbeck began the work he would continue throughout his life, seeking out and communicating with students, writers, and scholars from other countries and acting as a literary ambassador for the United States.

As he became more involved with the FIS, he decided to move to the East Coast, closer to Washington, DC, and further away from Carol, who remained in California. He and Gwyn moved to New York, first to a farmhouse north of Manhattan, and then to an apartment at the Bedford Hotel on East 14th Street in New York City. There he finished his first major work for the FIS, a novel called *The Moon is Down*. Inspired by his interviews with war refugees, Steinbeck created an unusual piece of propaganda. In its original version, it portrayed an American town occupied by Nazi troops.

A television adaptation of The Red Pony *starring Henry Fonda and Maureen O'Hara aired in 1973. It was a testament to Steinbeck's ability to create stories that continued to be relevant years after they were written.*

Since this first draft introduced the possibility of an American military defeat, the FIS refused to approve it. Steinbeck then revised his work, eventually locating the occupied town in northern Europe, rather than in the United States. But, despite this change, the publication of *The Moon is Down* initiated what some historians call "the fiercest literary battle of the Second World War."[16]

The Moon is Down weaves together the lives of ordinary people, politicians, and soldiers in a town occupied by foreign—implicitly Nazi—troops during World War II. The story ends where it begins, with the occupiers firmly entrenched in the town. But as the townspeople mount a resistance campaign, they prove that they will never submit to foreign rule and will ultimately win back their freedom. "You won't believe this," says Orden, the town's mayor, to the leaders of the occupation, "but it is true: authority is in the town. I don't know how or why, but it is so. This means we cannot act as quickly as you can, but when a direction is set, we all act together."[17] Orden asserts that democratic ideals, here resembling the group action of Steinbeck's phalanx, cannot be suppressed.

Steinbeck thought he had written an unambiguously patriotic book in *The Moon is Down,* so he was shocked when critics turned against him. Most objected to his depiction of the occupying forces. They argued that by making the Nazis appear too human—in the novel, the Nazi soldiers are frightened boys, not savages—Steinbeck would weaken the United States' will to fight. In a later essay, "My Short Novels," he explained his representation of the Nazis as a product of an honest evaluation: "I had written of Germans as men, not supermen, and this was considered a very weak attitude to take. I couldn't make much sense out of this, and it seems absurd now that we know the Germans were men, and thus fallible, even defeatable."[18] In 1941, however, the critics refused to accept this kind of reasoning and questioned his dedication to the American war effort.

Fortunately, the reading public understood *The Moon is Down* better than the critics. When the novel appeared in March 1942, it was a Book-of-the-Month Club main selection and sold more than 200,000 copies. A stage adaptation ran for nine weeks on Broadway, took second place in the competition for the New York Drama Critics' best play award, and then enjoyed long, successful runs in London and Stockholm. Underground agents in Norway secretly published the book to help improve morale in occupied villages, proving that the novel was a realistic account of life in an oc-

A still photo from the movie version of The Moon is Down, *one of Steinbeck's most controversial works*

cupied nation. The Nazis reportedly executed anyone found carrying a copy.[19] Still, by mid-1942, even Steinbeck recognized the flaws in *The Moon is Down,* and particularly in the stage presentation. In one letter, he wrote of the play, "It was dull. For some reason, probably because of my writing, it didn't come over the footlights."[20]

Dull or not, *The Moon is Down* was the right story at the right time. The novel was a bestseller; the play was influential at home and abroad; and Twentieth Century-Fox bought the movie rights for a record $300,000. But the money could not satisfy Steinbeck's real need in 1942: to write another major work, one worthy of the expectations he created for himself with *The Grapes of Wrath.*

CHAPTER FIVE

BATTLES

There is only one way to prove myself. I will ride on quest and let my actions speak for me. Words can be traitors but deeds have no advocate.

—*from* The Acts of King Arthur and His Noble Knights[1]

IN THE EARLY SPRING OF 1942, Steinbeck and Gwyn moved to Sneden's Landing in upstate New York, a quieter spot than Manhattan's Bedford Hotel. There, Steinbeck continued his work for the FIS, writing patriotic scripts for government radio broadcasts. In May, President Roosevelt called on Steinbeck to write a short book about the nation's air force. Steinbeck wanted to begin a new novel but he refused to disappoint his president during wartime. He agreed to visit twenty airfields in as many states to report on the training of bomber crews preparing for war. He spent a full month with pilots and soldiers, sleeping in barracks, eating army food, flying in warplanes and working on a manuscript eventually published as *Bombs Away: The Story of a Bomber Team.* As with several earlier books, *Bombs Away* became the object of a Hollywood bidding war, and Steinbeck eventually earned $250,000 for the movie rights. Already living comfortably, he donated the money from *Bombs Away* to the Air Force Aid Society Trust Fund and moved to Sherman Oaks, California, to oversee the production of the film.

But production languished. Steinbeck, who accepted this project simply because his president asked him to, found himself living in the suburbs of Los Angeles, away from Gwyn and with nothing to do. To make matters worse, officials in nearby Monterey were still angry over Steinbeck's support of the migrant farmers and threatened to draft him into the army as a combat soldier, despite the fact that he was forty years old. To pass the time, he collaborated with his friend Jack Wagner on a movie script called "A Medal for Benny." The story of a *paisano* who wins the Congressional Medal of Honor for bravery but dies on the battlefield, and of the girlfriend and father he leaves behind, "A Medal for Benny" inspired a weak film released in 1945. As he finished "A Medal for Benny," he took on several minor jobs, raising money for wartime charities and drafting a script for a musical titled "The Wizard of Maine," which traced the life of a con artist and magician who performs good works. He amused himself with "The Wizard of Maine" over the next three years but he never devoted his complete attention to the project.

He did complete a movie script for director Alfred Hitchcock, however. He based his script, "Lifeboat," on the true story of Eddie Rickenbacker, a legendary American pilot who escaped a sinking submarine, along with seven other soldiers, only to float in a rubber raft in the Pacific Ocean for twenty-four days. Twentieth Century-Fox rushed the film into production with encouragement from the U.S. Maritime Commission, but Steinbeck detested the final product, released in 1944. His original draft realistically portrayed the difficulties that Rickenbacker and the others had faced. And, as with so much of his previous and future work, he positioned the lifeboat as a kind of laboratory for human interaction. He filled his boat with many different kinds of people in order to investigate his ideas about the way society works. But Hitchcock did not share Steinbeck's interests. The brash director altered the script to conform to popular Hollywood stereotypes: a woman onboard complains about breaking a fingernail; a black character, whom Steinbeck had described as a hero, proves to be a thief; and a Nazi character appears as a superhuman fighter, despite Steinbeck's own rejection of that image in *The Moon is Down.* Steinbeck swore he would never work with Hitchcock again.[2]

Meanwhile, Gwyn began to lose patience with Steinbeck's frequent absences and his domineering personality. Home in New York in early 1943, living in a brownstone apartment on East 51st Street, he insisted that Gwyn give up her career as an entertainer and become a more conventional housewife. Gwyn agreed to honor Steinbeck's demands, but only temporarily; she could not live in Steinbeck's shadow for long. On March 29, after the finalization of his divorce from Carol, John married Gwyn at a friend's house in New Orleans. Like the marriage to follow, the wedding proved to be a disaster. Gwyn lost her wedding ring, the wedding cake arrived late to the reception, and the few friends in attendance, including the minister who performed the ceremony, drank too much alcohol. More trouble followed.

For months, Steinbeck had been negotiating with editors at the New York *Herald Tribune* to cover the war in Europe. The only reason he was not already reporting was that army counterintelligence agents, who ran background checks on all war correspondents, dug up old accusations from Steinbeck's California enemies who linked the writer to Communist organizations. Ironically, the same men who tried to draft Steinbeck into combat a year earlier were now convincing the federal government to deny him a passport. This harassment continued through April. Then in May, after the Monterey draft board abandoned its campaign against the writer, Steinbeck reacted poorly to pre-travel vaccinations and was confined to his bed for three weeks. Finally in June, just three months after his wedding and after his wife pleaded with him to stay in the United States—"How can you do this to me?" she cried[3]—he sailed to England.

Though he had worked as a journalist in the past, Steinbeck had little reporting experience when he entered the theater of war in 1943. Wisely, he befriended battle-hardened veterans such as Ernie Pyle, the most influential reporter covering the frontlines; Edward R. Murrow, the pioneer of broadcast journalism; and Robert Capa, the rogue photographer who created some of the war's most lasting images. Like Pyle, Steinbeck decided to live with the troops and study the war from the inside. Also like Pyle, he wrote human-interest stories, articles about the lives of the soldiers he met. He provided American newspaper readers with unique insights into troop life, and he presented them with a sense of humor as well as a sense of dark tragedy. "[E]ach man, in this last night in the moonlight, looks strangely at the others and sees death there," he wrote in one of his most powerful dispatches, composed on the eve of battle. "This is the most terrible time of all. This night before the assault by the new green troops. They will never be like this again."[4] For four months in 1943, few journalists wrote any better, to wider acclaim, or reached a larger audience. Steinbeck's syndicated articles appeared in England and in every state except Oklahoma, where newspaper editors still objected to his portrayal of the Okies.

Predictably, Steinbeck refused to be a passive observer of the fighting, and he did not avoid dangerous assignments. After meeting Douglas Fairbanks Jr., the Hollywood actor who commanded a PT boat in the Mediterranean, Steinbeck agreed to accompany Fairbanks's troops on a perilous mission off the coast of Italy. Fooling the Germans into believing he led more troops than the small PT boat could hold, Fairbanks landed on the island of Ventotene and, with Steinbeck by his side, took control of the German fortifications there. Fairbanks earned a Silver Star for his heroics and nominated Steinbeck for an award as well. "John, to his everlasting glory and our everlasting respect, would take his foreign correspondent badge off his arm and join the raid," Fairbanks remembered years later. "If you are caught in belligerent action without a badge and carrying a weapon, and you are a foreign correspondent, you are shot. . . . He took his risks rather than going along, saying grace as a war correspondent. We had a great admiration for him."[5] As a civilian, Steinbeck was ineligible for military honors, but he learned that he could survive the pressures of war as well as anyone.

On October 15, 1943, Steinbeck returned to Gwyn in New York. By all accounts, he was a changed man. As a result of his exposure to combat, he suffered two burst eardrums, a twisted ankle, a strained back, lumps on his head, temporary blackouts, and memory loss. And he suffered emotionally as well. One friend remembered, "The war shook him up. He had seen some things that hurt him. This was clear from his eyes, which had a faraway look in them, a kind of vacancy that frightened all of us."[6] Haunted by memories of the war, he grew irritable and argumentative and began to doubt the wisdom and goodness of human beings.

To revive his spirits, he started another short book about the *paisanos*, a sequel to *Tortilla Flat.* He claimed he was writing for the soldiers he met, who had asked him for something lighthearted and funny.[7] But in January 1944, he put that book on hold in order to repair his marriage. He and Gwyn traveled by car from New York to Mexico. In addition to spending much needed time with his wife, he read Mexican folktales and drafted a folktale of his own, *The Pearl,* a story he first heard during his journey with Ed Ricketts on the *Western Flyer.*

Written in a clear, simple style that fits its subject matter perfectly, *The Pearl* is the story of Kino, a fisherman who struggles to support his wife Juana and his son Coyotito. One morning Kino finds the tremendous

"Pearl of the World" at the bottom of a bay and, without any business experience, tries to sell it for a fair price. Sensing that city merchants are mistreating him, he ventures into Mexico to find a buyer only to fall prey to greedy villagers and agents of the merchants. After thieves accidentally kill his son, Kino returns to the shore and throws the pearl back into the waves, renouncing the bad luck it carries.

John intended to write *The Pearl* as a folktale about justice and honor in the face of adversity. But by focusing reader attention on Juana and Coyotito as well as Kino, he transformed the story into a parable about family and survival. The latter were the most important issues to him in early 1944—Gwyn was pregnant. On August 2, she gave birth to their first son, Thom. The boy's arrival changed his parents' lives more than they expected. John had grown used to writing in absolute silence, and Gwyn enjoyed an independent lifestyle. But Thom cried often and required constant care. As a result, Steinbeck's early descriptions of his son are less than enthusiastic. "I see nothing remarkable in this child at all," he wrote shortly after Thom's birth. "He's going to be reasonably pleasant looking and he has all his members and is healthy. . . . Neither of us are gaga but we're very glad to have him and we'll have some more."[8]

Despite serious reservations about fatherhood, Steinbeck adapted to his new responsibilities and moved back to Monterey so that his son could grow up in the country. Monterey officials continued their hostility toward Steinbeck and his family, however, maintaining the grudges that began with the publication of *In Dubious Battle*. The city refused to grant him permits to make repairs on his new home, temporarily cut off his gas supply, and prohibited him from renting office space for his writing. His relations with Monterey officials deteriorated further after Viking published the new *paisano* book, *Cannery Row,* in January 1945.

Cannery Row recounts events in the life of Doc, a marine biologist modeled after Ed Ricketts and a friend to the hoboes and prostitutes who inhabit the industrial center of Monterey. Grateful for all of Doc's help in their lives, the residents of Cannery Row throw a party in his honor. Like the party in *Tortilla Flat,* it ends in fistfights and criminal behavior. But Doc, like Steinbeck, sees through his neighbors' brutishness and recognizes their great capacity for loyalty and friendship. "There are the true philosophers," Doc says about the residents of Cannery Row. "I think they survive in this particular world better than other people. In a time when people tear themselves to pieces with ambition and nervousness and covetousness, they are relaxed."[9]

Although *Cannery Row* contains several humorous passages and several important critiques of polite American society, few critics praised the book. Many considered it a retread of the more successful *Tortilla Flat.* "There just isn't much here," wrote Orville Prescott of the *New York Times*, "no real characters, no 'story,' no purpose."[10] The residents of Monterey responded even less favorably, objecting to Steinbeck's portrayal of their city as a center for prostitution, alcoholism, and homelessness. Rejected by his neighbors, Steinbeck once again left the region he loved. As he quit California for New York in the spring of 1945, he wrote to Pat Covici, "You remember how happy I was to come back here. It was really a home coming. Well there is no home coming nor any welcome. What there is is jealousy and hatred and the knife in the back. . . . This isn't my country anymore. And it won't be until I am dead. It makes me very sad."[11]

But for Steinbeck, the most painful rejection of *Cannery Row* came from his friends, like Covici, who began to doubt his abilities as a novelist. "[I] dipped into *Grapes of Wrath*," his editor wrote in early 1945. "The overture essays . . . what organ music they are. And I was thinking—please forgive me—when will you put your clarinet away (not that I don't enjoy its lovely lyric music) and take up the organ once again."[12] Covici was too polite and too concerned about his writer's emotional health to criticize Steinbeck directly. But John understood his message. Even if the American public continued to buy everything John wrote, Pat Covici, like most other critics, was losing patience with his recent string of minor books. It was time for another major effort.

CHAPTER SIX

VALLEYS

So many lives were about, and all with friends and enemies, that Sir Lancelot felt alone and lonely in his heart, darkened and chilled also, and no stars shone in him.

—*from* The Acts of King Arthur and His Noble Knights[1]

IN THE WINTER OF 1945, John and Gwyn toured Mexico and, for the first time, worked together on a project. While John revised the movie script of *The Pearl*, Gwyn researched Mexican folk music and planned the film's score. Film executives also asked Steinbeck if he would write a screenplay for a film about the Mexican freedom fighter Emiliano Zapata. Steinbeck had long been interested in Zapata, a champion of the poor and powerless—a real-life version of Tom Joad—but did not begin his research until he received assurances that the Mexican government would not interfere with his work. He had learned to protect himself after his battles with the Monterey businessmen and officials.

Throughout the first half of 1946, he shuttled between Mexico and a new house on East 78th Street in Manhattan, a brownstone with a garden. He and Gwyn also purchased the house next door. After living among the hostile residents of Monterey, Steinbeck wanted to make sure he knew and trusted his neighbors. He soon completed the repairs on both houses and rented the neighboring brownstone to Nathaniel Benchley, a writer for *Newsweek* and an aspiring novelist, and his wife Marjorie.

While in Mexico City in October, John learned that Gwyn was pregnant again. She visited him in November, but he was still too busy with the film of *The Pearl* and with his Zapata research to pay much attention to her. Only later in the year, when he finally returned to New York, did he care for her the way she wanted him to. He did not give up his writing entirely, however. He revised one of his old stories about Mexico, "*El camión vacilador*," shifted the setting to southern California, and renamed it "The Wayward Bus." As Gwyn's health improved, Steinbeck gained momentum. He wrote 2,400 words a day, dictating his story into a tape recorder before committing it to the page.

On June 12, 1946, Gwyn gave birth to John Steinbeck IV, called Catbird by his proud but aloof father. Gwyn remained bedridden for two months after the birth, complaining of pains and fevers. Steinbeck, itching to resume his writing, cared for the infant and for Thom while he nursed his wife. Eventually, he began to doubt the severity of Gwyn's ailments and accused her of faking her sickness to capture his attention.

After nearly a year of nursing, parenting, and writing, Steinbeck accepted an invitation from his Danish publisher to visit Denmark. In October 1946, John and Gwyn flew to Sweden and took a train to Copenhagen, where the writer was greeted with a celebrity's welcome. "I didn't know anyone treated writers like this," he wrote to McIntosh and Otis. "It is the sort of thing that would greet [actress] Lana Turner if it became known that she was going to come into Grand Central Station without any clothes on."[2] Even more startling to John, however, Norway's King Haakon honored him with a Liberty Cross, a medal usually reserved for national war heroes. King Haakon officially recognized the importance of *The Moon is Down* to the Norwegian resistance movement and credited Steinbeck's work with helping the nation survive the Nazi invasion. After receiving the medal, Steinbeck charmed the king with his blunt sense of humor. "Thank you," he said as the king bestowed the cross. "How much did this cost?"[3] Later, when reporters asked him how he could portray the resistance movement so accurately without witnessing that part of the war firsthand, Steinbeck responded, "I put myself in your place and thought what I would do."[4] Steinbeck enjoyed the praise he received from the Norwegians. He remembered how American critics rejected *The Moon is Down* even though they had never gotten close to the war.

But he could not savor this victory. He and Gwyn fought bitterly during this trip. Jealous of the attention her husband received, she insisted that they return to New York in late November despite their plans to visit London. In his moment of triumph, Steinbeck fell into yet another depression and started drinking heavily again.

Before leaving for Scandinavia, Steinbeck had finished *The Wayward Bus*, which appeared in February 1947. It was a guaranteed success even before it arrived in bookstores. The Book-of-the-Month Club sold 600,000 copies and Viking sold an additional 150,000 advance copies. It was Steinbeck's most successful book yet. According to the critics, however, *The Wayward Bus* was an almost complete failure. Some journals praised the spare writing style Steinbeck had developed, and many were pleased to see that he was approaching his characters from a less sentimental point of view. But nearly every critic rejected the book as a clumsy, failed allegory.

As he had attempted with "Lifeboat," Steinbeck treated the book as a laboratory for the study of human interaction and community. Gathering a variety of characters on a broken-down bus—a middle-class businessman and his family, a mysterious beauty, a starstruck waitress, a Chicano bus driver, and an adolescent boy—Steinbeck traced their evolving relationships. Like many of his previous works, *The Wayward Bus* contains harsh critiques of polite middle-class society and the nation's celebration of fame and beauty, but it never achieves the intensity or the unity of Steinbeck's best work. In 1947, such a failure seemed like more evidence that Steinbeck had lost his touch. Although he was as popular with the reading public as he had ever been, he knew that he was damaging his reputation with his most recent work.

He felt increasing pressure as a husband and father as well. In late February, after yet another loud argument with John, Gwyn ran away to California, taking the children with her. Steinbeck followed his family to Los Angeles and convinced Gwyn to return home. But now even he had to accept that their marriage was ending. As usual, he traveled to escape his problems. He convinced the editors of the New York *Herald Tribune* to fund a tour of the European continent, where he would report on changes since the end of World War II. But before he left New York he met with Robert Capa, the photographer he befriended during the war. Capa proposed that he and John embark on a very different adventure from the one Steinbeck planned. Instead of Europe, Capa wanted to visit the Soviet Union, a U.S. ally during World War II but rapidly becoming America's main antagonist in world politics. Dissatisfied with his home life and his writing, Steinbeck accepted Capa's proposal and traveled to Paris, the first stop on the way to the Soviet Union. He received a warm welcome from the Parisians, who seemed to appreciate *The Wayward Bus* more than American critics, and he and Gwyn spent a few weeks together in the City of Lights before he left for Moscow.

Although Steinbeck and Capa were world famous, no one greeted them upon their arrival in the Soviet capital. For weeks, Soviet officials confined them to the city, prohibiting their movement around the countryside. But by mid-August they were allowed to visit the Ukraine. They met with politicians, peasants, and professionals. Typical for Steinbeck, who had humanized America's enemies in *The Moon is Down,* he wrote in his published account of the journey, *The Russian Journal,* that he and Capa had found "that the Russian people are people, and, as with other people, that they are very nice.

The ones we met had a hatred of war, they wanted the same things all people want—good lives, increased comfort, security, and peace."[5] However fair and modest this conclusion may seem, such a defense of Russian life drew intense criticism from Americans in the early days of the Cold War.

While Steinbeck was in Russia, Viking released *The Pearl* to coincide with the movie adaptation released by RKO. For the most part, critics ignored both the book and the film. But, this time, Steinbeck's story did not even appeal to the general public. Despite the true beauty of Steinbeck's language and the nobility of the simple plot, most considered *The Pearl* naive, melodramatic, and too flimsy a work for a once-great author. Few recognized the strengths and virtues that would eventually make *The Pearl* one of the most beloved of Steinbeck's works. When John returned from Russia in December—after stopovers in Prague and Budapest—he faced more hostile reviews and another literary failure. In addition, he fought again with Gwyn, who claimed to be too sick to take care of the boys and would not let him finish his articles on the recent trip.

By January, he was running from Gwyn again. This time, he traveled back to Salinas to begin research on a novel he had been planning for years. Earlier, in 1945, his sister Beth had given him a box containing John Adolph Grosssteinbeck's personal papers, including the records of his grandfather's experiences in Jerusalem and Florida. This find inspired Steinbeck to write his family history and the history of the Salinas Valley. Now, in early 1948, he spent his days at the Salinas library, poring over old newspapers. "I am on my marathon book, which is called Salinas Valley" he wrote to a friend early in his research. "It is what I have been practicing to write all my life. Everything else has been training. . . . I wouldn't even care if it took all the rest of my life if I got it done."[6] But even as he began the long "marathon" of writing and research, Steinbeck grew restless and considered other, more immediate ways to reach an audience. With Capa, actor Burgess Meredith, director Elia Kazan, and others, he organized World Video, a television production company for RKO. John even wrote a script for a show about the clothing industry. But the entire project was doomed from the start. None of the participants knew anything about the growing television industry. Although he was disappointed when World Video collapsed, and lost a lot of his own money, Steinbeck was lucky that the company collapsed when it did. His life was about to get complicated once again.

In April, he underwent surgery to remove painful varicose veins from his legs. At the same time, Gwyn was hospitalized with a sinus infection. But the worst news came in early May. Ed Ricketts had been involved in a terrible accident in Monterey. Ed often let his possessions fall into disrepair, and his car—a Packard with a loud, grinding engine—was in particularly bad shape. On May 7, the engine roared so loudly he could not hear a train approaching as he crossed the railroad tracks and collided with the Del Monte Express. Steinbeck rushed to Monterey but Ed died on May 11, before John arrived. After Ed's funeral, John sorted through his friend's papers and found a safe in Ed's office. He called in a locksmith to open the safe, but all he found inside was a bottle of Scotch whiskey and a note: "What the hell do you expect to find in here? Here's a drink for your trouble."[7]

In a letter to a friend, later in the month, John wrote, "Ed Ricketts' car was hit by a train and after fighting for his life for three days he died, and there died the greatest man I have ever known and the best teacher. It is going to take a long time to reorganize my thinking and my planning without him."[8] As friend, partner, confidante, and inspiration, Ed had influenced every part of Steinbeck's life. Steinbeck depended on Ed for ideas and support. And now he felt alone.

When he returned to New York after Ed's funeral, his loneliness intensified. Gwyn told him what he had been waiting to hear for months: she wanted a divorce and she wanted him to move out of the house immediately. She knew she could not fulfill her aspirations while playing the role of John Steinbeck's wife. Steinbeck moved into the Bedford Hotel, and Gwyn and the boys moved back to California. She refused to communicate with him for some time.

Distraught over the end of his marriage and his separation from his sons, he abandoned "The Salinas Valley" and resumed work on his screenplay about Emiliano Zapata. The Zapata research presented Steinbeck with an opportunity to escape to Mexico once again. This time, however, he was sad, unstable, and seemed a danger to himself. McIntosh and Otis sent an employee to Mexico to check on their star writer. Her report on John's condition was discouraging, even frightening: "He is in a strange mood and has very peculiar ideas of women these days. He eats at odd hours and not properly, stays up late and sleeps late and tries hard to convince himself that he likes it."[9] Only his work on Zapata and, eventually, another woman, would help him overcome his depression.

Steinbeck had first considered writing about Zapata in 1940, while doing research for the documentary *The Forgotten Village.* Now, with the support of director Elia Kazan—Kazan, like Steinbeck, preferred stories about people fighting for justice—Steinbeck immersed himself in Zapata's life. In truth, he worked too hard on the script, wrote too much, and would soon have to cut most of what he submitted to Kazan. But the Zapata project became a personal statement for Steinbeck. With his best friend dead and his wife gone, Steinbeck asked himself whether a man, friendless and alone, could continue to live a valuable life and still be a hero. [10]

He found his answer in the short life of Zapata. A young peasant from the Mexican countryside, Emiliano Zapata grew up during a violent period of Mexican history. Between 1867 and 1913, the nation suffered four bloody revolutions. In 1914, Zapata led the peasant armies who took back the government from a military tyrant. After his victory, Zapata was betrayed and assassinated by a government agent who objected to his growing influence. But his memory continued to inspire rural Mexicans as they fought corrupt, oppressive governments. In time, Steinbeck became an expert on Mexico's various revolutions, but his interest in Zapata surpassed that of a historian. In Zapata, he found the kind of hero he had admired as a boy reading the tales of King Arthur. He even worried that Zapata was too perfect to make an interesting character. "Zapata's life was devotion to an idea that never changed," he wrote in his first text on the rebel leader. "And this makes him unbelievable. Character on stage is usually a balance of weaknesses and strengths, but this man had practically no weaknesses. Therefore, he has practically no character dramatically."[11] Steinbeck's challenge was to present his hero in a way that would attract moviegoers who did not share his enthusiasm for political and social reformers.

By the late fall, Steinbeck had reasserted control of his life. His new alimony and child-support payments forced him into debt, but he knew he could make most of that money back again. He was no longer drinking so heavily. He once again moved into the family house in Pacific Grove. And he received word in early December that he had been elected to the prestigious American Academy of Arts and Letters. Weary of rejection, Steinbeck accepted the Academy's praise modestly. "Having been blackballed from everything from the Boy Scouts to the United States Army," he wrote to the electors of the Academy, "this election is not only a great experience but for me a unique one."[12]

Slowly, Steinbeck regained confidence in himself as a writer and a person. While reworking the Zapata screenplay in Pacific Grove—and writing a series of short stories about fatherhood—he started dating again and became a frequent subject of newspaper gossip columns. First, he was spotted with actress Paulette Goddard, who had once dated Charlie Chaplin and would later marry Burgess Meredith. Then newspapers linked him to actress Ann Sothern. And then Sothern introduced him to Elaine Scott. John immediately fell in love with Sothern's pretty, less-glamorous friend. "It was a little embarrassing," Elaine remembered years later, "because it was pretty obvious that he was interested in me, not

Ann. The relationship just worked . . . right from the start."[13] Elaine was married at the time but had separated from her husband. So Steinbeck wrote several letters inquiring about her: "I like Annie [Sothern]. She's a nice girl. And she was thoroughly chaperoned by Mrs. Zachary Scott. . . . As a matter of fact I kind of fell for the Scott girl. Who is she—do you know? I mean who was she? She was with the Theatre Guild. Can you give me a report on her?"[14]

The "Scott girl" was born Elaine Anderson, the daughter of an oil executive from Fort Worth, Texas. She attended the University of Texas as a drama major, married actor and occasional leading man Zachary Scott, worked as stage manager in a number of Broadway plays including the first production of *Oklahoma!*, and was the mother of a young girl, Waverly. Self-confident, quick-witted, and tough-minded, she proved a perfect match for Steinbeck. Their relationship developed quickly.

In the summer of 1949, Steinbeck rented a beach house near Malibu, California, where he spent three months with his sons, rewriting the Zapata script in the morning and playing with Thom and John all day. He wanted to reverse some of the harmful lessons he thought his sons were learning from their mother; he wanted to teach them to be brave, rugged men. Although Thom was only four years old and Catbird was two, their father had big plans for them. "They are going to eat when they are hungry and sleep when they are sleepy," he wrote to a friend. "As much as possible they are going to be responsible for their actions."[15] He even suggested that the boys learn how to drive cars, sail boats, and fly airplanes. But as much as he wanted to be a good father, he never learned how to connect with his boys. He expected too much of them, never gave them enough of his attention, and perhaps never realized that his own fame could be a burden to them.

Steinbeck was more successful in other areas of his life that summer. Elaine and Waverly visited frequently, and he was writing well again. He resumed work on the Salinas Valley novel, began a new play-novella he called "In the Forest of the Night," and finished his life of Zapata.

Since the first draft of the Zapata project ran several hundred pages too long, producer Darryl Zanuck

John Steinbeck with sons Thom (center) and Catbird

hired writer-producer Jules Buck to help Steinbeck mold it into shape. After four weeks of successful collaboration, they finished the screenplay for the movie, soon to be called *Viva Zapata!* The film became the most idealistic, socially conscious work Steinbeck had attempted since *The Grapes of Wrath*, with speeches that rival those of Tom Joad and Jim Casey. "Our cause was land," declares one of Zapata's soldiers as the revolution draws to an end. "Not a thought, but corn-planted earth to feed the families. And Liberty—not a word, but a man sitting safely in front of his house in the evening. And Peace—not a dream, but a time of rest and kindness."[16] In such passages, Steinbeck regained his nerve and his willingness to tackle broad social issues in his writing. He seemed to be regaining his voice.

In the late fall, John and Elaine rented separate apartments in a building on East 52nd Street in New York, where he completed "In the Forest of the Night," soon to be published as *Burning Bright.* He then convinced the legendary Broadway writing team, Richard Rodgers and Oscar Hammerstein, to produce a stage version of the novella. *Burning Bright* was a strange choice for the popular producers: an experimental play about a man who doubts his self-worth because he has failed to father a child. Through this novella, Steinbeck explored the issues that were haunting him: fatherhood, his legacy, and human relationships. But he wrote in deliberately stilted language, and he staged the three-act play in three different settings: first the characters are circus performers, then farmers, and finally sailors. He employed these techniques to give the novella and play a special quality, as he explained a year after the play's debut: "The attempt was to lift the story to the parable expression of the morality plays. It is a method not without its great exponents."[17] Unfortunately, his stylistic experiments did not work. The novel version of *Burning Bright* met resistance from book clubs because of its odd stylistic elements and its explicitly sexual content. The stage version closed after only eleven performances in the summer of 1950.

During the next year, Viking published *The Log from the Sea of Cortez*, the narrative portion of the *Sea of Cortez* written primarily by Steinbeck. In addition, Covici and poet Carl Sandburg convinced Steinbeck to collect and republish his wartime dispatches under the title *Once There Was a War.* Both books received positive reviews and sold modestly, but they did not satisfy Steinbeck's desire for another important book. They were old pieces of writing, after all. He came to realize that the Salinas Valley book, the one he had been planning and researching for years, would either save or destroy his reputation.

CHAPTER SEVEN

UNDEFEATED

Now that the battle had fixed Arthur more nearly in his kingship, many great lords and ladies came to do him homage.

—*from* The Acts of King Arthur and His Noble Knights[1]

JOHN MARRIED ELAINE on December 28, 1950, in the home of his publisher, Harold Guinzburg. After a one-week honeymoon in Bermuda and a short trip to Hollywood to check on the production of *Viva Zapata!*, the Steinbecks settled into their new house at 206 East 72nd Street. And John settled into his work on "The Salinas Valley."

He now thought of the book as a gift to his sons. Thom and Catbird were growing up under difficult conditions; their father, the famous writer, did not take an active role in their lives while their mother, Gwyn,

Elaine and John Steinbeck

seemed psychologically and emotionally unstable. John hoped that "The Salinas Valley," partially based on Steinbeck and Hamilton family lore, would give the boys some sense of their heroic ancestors and teach them the lessons John could not teach them face-to-face.

As he completed sections of the book, he sent weekly installments to Pat Covici. In addition to the text of the novel, he also sent Pat his journal entries from the week, which included his thoughts on his family, friends, and the writing process. He relied on Pat for research and writing supplies as well as emotional support. But John's dependence on Pat placed the editor in a difficult position. Torn between his roles as John's editor and his friend, Pat mostly encouraged John's work and depended on others to tell him about problems in his writing. In the long run, John's inability to accept criticism and Pat's inability to criticize John's work resulted in a series of novels that never fulfilled their potential. And if Elaine and Elizabeth Otis had not spoken up about the weaknesses in "The Salinas Valley," it would have suffered the same fate.

John worked through the summer of 1951. By November, he had produced nearly 265,000 words. He placed a thick, completed manuscript in a mahogany box and sent it to Pat with a note that would become the book's dedication: "Well, here's your box. Nearly everything I have is in it, and it is not full. Pain and excitement are in it, and feeling good or bad and evil thoughts and good thoughts—the pleasure of design and some despair and the indescribable joy of creation."[2] As the note suggests, the novel had grown in John's mind from a narrative about his childhood home to a tale of epic proportions. He had been trying to write a large, important novel since the publication of *The Grapes of Wrath.* So after a number of false starts and failures, he finally decided to try something daring and bold with his Salinas Valley novel. "In utter loneliness a writer tries to explain the inexplicable," he wrote in his journal. "And if he is a writer wise enough to know it can't be done, then he is not a writer at all. A good writer always works at the impossible."[3] To Steinbeck, working "at the impossible" meant exploring the most important subject he could think of: the struggle between good and evil. He restructured his new work around the biblical story of Cain and Abel, and renamed it *East of Eden.*

In *East of Eden,* Steinbeck wove together three separate narratives: the history of the Salinas Valley, the history of the Hamilton family—most notably Steinbeck's maternal grandfather Samuel Hamilton—and the fictional story of Adam Trask, his wife Cathy, and sons Caleb and Aaron. When Cathy abandons the family for a life of prostitution in King City, Adam withdraws from society and forces his sons to learn the truth about their mother on their own. And neither Samuel Hamilton nor the Trask family's Chinese cook, Lee, can save the boys from tragedy. But Steinbeck's novel reaches beyond the confines of the Salinas Valley to comment on the presence of evil in American society as a whole. In one episode, Lee suggests that a nation settled by immigrants must always be a violent place:

> *We're a violent people. . . . Maybe it's true that we are all descended from the restless, the nervous, the criminals, the arguers and brawlers, but also the*

> *brave and independent and generous. If our ancestors had not been that, they would have stayed in their home plots in the other world and starved over the squeezed-out soil.*[4]

And it is Lee again, as the novel's central voice of wisdom, who suggests that the only way for human beings to defeat evil is through *timshel*, a Hebrew word for the freedom to choose right from wrong. "Why, that makes a man great," Lee says. "That gives him stature with the gods, for in his weakness and his filth and his murder of his brother he has still the great choice. He can choose his course and fight it through and win."[5]

Few twentieth century writers had chosen to confront issues of good and evil as directly as Steinbeck in *East of Eden,* so no one knew how readers would respond when the book arrived in stores in September 1952. To John's relief, *East of Eden* soared to the top of most bestseller lists even though the Book-of-the-Month Club rejected it for its frank discussion of prostitution. Despite his recent failures, he had not lost his audience. But reviewers were more conflicted about the value of the book. Typically, they attacked his representation of Cathy, whose evil nature they deemed unbelievable. But they also acknowledged and praised Steinbeck's courage in attempting such an ambitious novel. Most reviewers echoed Orville Prescott of the *New York Times*, who struggled with the novel's many contradictions: "Clumsy in structure and defaced by excessive melodramatics and much cheap sensationalism though it is, *East of Eden* is a serious and on the whole a successful effort to grapple with a major theme."[6] Such praise, though qualified, convinced John that he had succeeded in writing an important book. More confident about his place in literary history, and with Elaine by his side, he was happier than he had ever been in his life.

Before the book's publication, John sought new projects to occupy his time and shield him from the press. First, he worked for the presidential campaign of Adlai Stevenson, the Democratic governor of Illinois who ran against General Dwight D. Eisenhower, the hero of World War II. Stevenson's rational and intellectual approach to the campaign appealed to the Steinbecks. Elaine helped organize Stevenson rallies while John worked as a consultant, offering Stevenson speech ideas and writing some speeches for Stevenson supporters. But Eisenhower, the war hero, captured the hearts of Americans and defeated Stevenson in a landslide victory.

In March, John and Elaine left for Europe. John arranged to work as an editor-at-large for *Collier's* magazine, writing the same kinds of human-interest stories he mastered during the war. For the first three months of the journey, he published no articles. Later, he increased his production only slightly. In truth, events back home distracted Steinbeck from his work. Elia Kazan called to tell him that *Viva Zapata!* was a hit, earning more than $3 million in its first month in theaters. The film succeeded despite several obstacles, including poor filming conditions and resistance from the Mexican government. In addition, Kazan became the target of a U.S. government investigation, when the House Un-American Activities Committee (HUAC) researched his involvement with socialist and communist organizations. For years, Steinbeck had been the subject of similar investigations by California state officials, but Kazan faced the full power of the federal government and cooperated with HUAC, naming other former communists in the film industry. The controversy over Kazan's testimony reached John in Rome, where a communist paper, *L'Unita*, criticized Steinbeck for supporting Kazan. John believed he was merely helping a friend; he hated HUAC's persecutions, and he supported another acquaintance, playwright Arthur Miller, when Miller refused to cooperate with the committee. Fortunately, the controversy did not detract from the popularity of *Viva Zapata!* Actor Marlon Brando was nominated for an Academy Award for his portrayal of Zapata. Composer Alex North was nominated for writing the movie's score. Anthony Quinn won the best-supporting-actor award for his portrayal of Zapata's brother Eufemio. And Steinbeck received his third Oscar nomination for best screenplay. (He had also been nominated for *Lifeboat* and *A Medal for Benny*.)

Home again in 1953, after failing to produce any first-rate articles for *Collier's*, Steinbeck searched for a new project. For a short time he tried to transform *Cannery Row* into a Broadway musical, but abandoned that idea in favor of writing another novel about the poor residents of Monterey. He stayed in Manhattan to work on the novel through the summer. Only in September, as it neared completion, did he finally leave the sweltering heat of the city for a beach house at Sag Harbor, in eastern Long Island. By that time, he knew that Rodgers and Hammerstein would adapt the new novel,

Marlon Brando (right) starred as Emiliano Zapata in the 1952 film Viva Zapata!

ultimately called *Sweet Thursday,* into a major Broadway production.

Both the characters and the plot of *Sweet Thursday* were familiar to Steinbeck's fans. As in *Cannery Row,* the residents of the flophouses and shacks throw Doc a costume party, this time hoping to introduce him to a woman, a sharp-witted prostitute, who will make his life less lonely. After the long, arduous work on *East of Eden, Sweet Thursday* presented Steinbeck with an opportunity to clear his head and lose himself in the scenarios that gave him so much enjoyment. Returning to "cannery row" had always been good for his state of mind—if not his writing. In addition, the novel gave him an opportunity to finish the story of Doc and to say goodbye to Ed Ricketts through the character that Ed inspired. In the final scene of *Sweet Thursday*, Doc (and Ed) ride off into the sunset in a proper hero's farewell:

> *Doc turned in the seat and looked back. The disappearing sun shone on his laughing face, his gay eager face. With his left hand, he held the bucking steering wheel. Cannery Row looked after the ancient car. It made the first turn and was gone from sight behind a warehouse just as the sun was gone.*[7]

With that scene, John wrote his own ending to an important chapter in his life and finally learned to accept Ed's death as well as his own advancing age.

Shortly after completing the manuscript of *Sweet Thursday*, Steinbeck complained of a weakness in his hands. He spent ten days in Lenox Hill Hospital during the late fall, undergoing a series of physical and psychological tests. At the time no one suspected that he was suffering the effects of a series of minor strokes. Doctors assumed instead that John was tired and overworked. So he and Elaine took several vacations, first to St. John in the Caribbean and then to Europe. In Paris in the spring of 1954, John collapsed again. This time, doctors mistakenly diagnosed his illness as sunstroke. While recovering from this latest attack, he wrote a series of articles for the French weekly magazine *Figaro littéraire*. The work boosted his spirits, until he learned that his friend Robert Capa had died while reporting on the war raging in the French colony of Vietnam. In poor health himself, Steinbeck reacted badly to Capa's death. Although he and Elaine continued to travel across the European continent and were repeatedly greeted as celebrities wherever they went, little could significantly alter his sad mood—not the news that *Sweet Thursday* received good reviews and sold well, and not the news that Elia Kazan had finished work on the movie version of *East of Eden*, with James Dean starring as Cal Trask.

The 1955 film version of East of Eden *starred James Dean.*

Returning to the States just before Christmas, John determined to make some changes in his life and to revive his interest in writing. In February 1955, he purchased a house in Sag Harbor, Long Island, New York, on a two-acre plot beside a cove. He accepted a job as editor-at-large for the *Saturday Review*, for which he would write articles about contemporary American culture and politics. And, for the first time in years, he experimented with his writing style. "I want to dump my technique," he wrote to Elizabeth Otis, "to tear it right down to the ground and to start all over."[8] Through 1955, he tinkered with word sounds and syntax as well as a variety of story ideas, including an attempt at science fiction. But he was too easily distracted by his surroundings at Sag Harbor—birds, boats, fish—to focus on his writing. He was also distracted by the Broadway production of *Sweet Thursday*, which Rodgers and Hammerstein had renamed *Pipe Dream*. Like Alfred Hitchcock a decade earlier, the producers turned Steinbeck's unusual novel into a more conventional story about two people in love, and John had little patience for the producers' revisions. In a letter to Hammerstein, expressing his frustration with the show, he wrote, "When *Oklahoma* came out, it violated every conventional rule of Musical Comedy. . . . But Oscar, time has moved. The form has moved. You can't stand still."[9] Despite Steinbeck's warnings, however, Rodgers and Hammerstein refused to present the racier aspects of the story and the show received a lukewarm reception in New York. Steinbeck finally gave up his ambition to write for the stage and vacationed in the Caribbean in order to escape the negative press that followed *Pipe Dream*'s debut.

When he returned to Sag Harbor, he wrote a short story for *Atlantic Monthly*, "How Mr. Hogan Robbed a Bank," about what he perceived as a general moral decline in American society. This story marked a shift in his interests and presaged the strangest novel in his entire body of work, a sociopolitical satire about the return of monarchy to France. Shuttling between Manhattan and eastern Long Island, he could not find the peace he needed to complete the novel to his satisfaction. During their visits, Thom and Catbird demanded his attention, while Elaine was busy preparing for her daughter's wedding. Foul-tempered and angry, he completed a first draft of the novel, *The Short Reign of Pippin IV,* in April and shipped it off to Pat Covici. Then he prepared for a new reporting assignment: the editors of the *St. Louis Courier-Journal* had hired him to cover the upcoming presidential conventions.

The Democratic convention took place in Chicago in early August. To John's satisfaction, the man he had supported four years earlier, Adlai Stevenson, once again won the party's nomination. He channeled his enthusiasm for Stevenson into the kind of folksy journalism he been writing since World War II. More experienced reporters marveled at Steinbeck's eagerness to learn the new trade. "Steinbeck was like a cub reporter," one journalist remembered. "Enthusiastic, tentative, eager to please us. He threw himself into this reporting in a way that surprised everyone. The pieces he wrote were anecdotal, full of wry observations. . . . He was a novelist, so he made little short stories of what he saw, and he saw a lot."[10] When the *Courier-Journal* syndicated Steinbeck's articles, readers of forty different newspapers around the country came to see the conventions through Steinbeck's eyes. After President Eisenhower and Vice President Richard Nixon were renominated at the Republican convention in San Francisco, Steinbeck devoted his energies to the new Stevenson campaign. But, once again, Stevenson lost the general election in November.

Home from the conventions in the early fall, John learned that Pat Covici, Elizabeth Otis, and most editors at Viking disliked the manuscript of *The Short Reign of Pippin IV.* Pat encouraged him to abandon the satire and turn his attention to short stories. But John insisted that Viking publish the novel as it stood. Reviewers offered fewer criticisms than Steinbeck's friends, though they typically expressed confusion about how Steinbeck could write a book so different from *The Grapes of Wrath.* And, as usual, the book sold well. But the plot—following the life of Pippin Héristal, an absent-minded astronomer who becomes the new king of France—and the book's flat humor suggested a change in Steinbeck's approach. He had, of course, written about politics indirectly throughout his career. But *The Short Reign of Pippin IV* represented Steinbeck's new determination to write directly about political philosophy. He had found a new subject, but he had not found his new voice.

In November 1956, John thought he discovered the proper vehicle for his renewed interest in social and political causes: the legend of King Arthur. The idea was not his own. A New York bookseller, Chase Horton from the Washington Square Bookshop, had learned of Steinbeck's interest in King Arthur and encouraged him to update the legend for the modern age. Horton even promised to help Steinbeck with his research. John accepted Horton's challenge. He had always asserted that Sir Thomas Malory's *Le Morte d'Arthur* had formed his sense of right and wrong.[11] By rewriting the Malory text and updating its fifteenth-century language, Steinbeck hoped to convey his beliefs to future generations of Americans. But as he began his research, Steinbeck became so fascinated by the mysterious character of Malory himself that his project changed. Now, one famous writer struggled to understand the life and work of another famous writer.

Meanwhile, since his work for magazines and newspapers made him a respected social commentator, several national and international organizations requested his support. He joined eminent writers such as William Faulkner, William Carlos Williams, and Saul Bellow on a committee organized by the Eisenhower administration to increase communication between the United States and the Soviet Union. Traveling through Europe in 1957, he represented the United States Information Service, helping to improve relationships between U.S. embassies and European governments. He traveled to Stockholm, Sweden, to have dinner with Dag Hammarskjöld, the secretary-general of the United Nations. And in August 1957, he attended a conference of the International Association of Poets, Playwrights, Editors, Essayists and Novelists (PEN) held in Tokyo. The world press mobbed him when he arrived, and conference organizers asked him to deliver a speech to close the first day's festivities.

Back in the States in December, he resumed his Malory research, which he continued intermittently through 1958. But his work on Malory ground to a halt in June, when he read critic Alfred Kazin's reevaluation of his novels in the *New York Times Book Review*. Kazin charged that Steinbeck had not written anything valuable since *The Grapes of Wrath.* Many critics agreed with Kazin's criticism—even Pat Covici hinted that the quality of John's work diminished after *The Grapes of Wrath*—but few people ever stated their objections so directly. Kazin's critique crushed the self-confidence Steinbeck had been building since *East of Eden.* In response, he turned from the King Arthur stories to a modern adaptation of Miguel de Cervantes's classic *Don Quixote.* He hoped the adaptation, which he called "Don Keehan," would tackle large themes and thereby refute Kazin's criticism. But by Christmas, he admitted to Covici that "Don Keehan" was an inferior project:

> *Frankly this is a hack book and I'm not ready for that yet. To be a writer implies a kind of promise that one will do the best he can without reference to external pressures of any kind. . . . And only insofar as I can be a more brutal critic than anyone around me, can I deserve the rather proud status I have set up for myself and have not always maintained.*[12]

The pressure that Steinbeck now placed on himself to maintain his "proud status" as a writer led to his first serious case of writer's block.

To combat the writer's block, the Steinbecks traveled to Somerset, England, in March 1959 and moved into Discove Cottage, ten miles from the traditional location of King Arthur's castle, Camelot. In this quiet environment, Steinbeck rededicated himself to his translation of the Malory texts. He taught himself to write again. "My love and respect and homage for my language is coming back," he wrote to Elia Kazan in April. "Here are proud words and sharp words and words as dainty as little girls and stone words needing no adjectives as crutches. And they join hands and dance beauty on the paper."[13] After a short time at Discove Cottage, he produced enough manuscript pages to send some out to Covici, Otis, and Horton for comment. But their comments were not favorable. They considered John's translations dull and believed he made a mistake in taking on the project. John soldiered on, but without the support of his editors and friends he could not finish his translation. Elaine found the incomplete manuscript years later, after Steinbeck's death, and published it in 1976 as *The Acts of King Arthur and His Noble Knights.*

Home from Somerset in the fall of 1959, John suffered another attack similar to the strokes of 1953. Elaine was working in the kitchen of their Manhattan apartment when she smelled smoke. She found John lying in bed, unconscious, his pajamas smoldering beneath a lit cigarette that dropped from his hand. When he regained consciousness, his speech was slurred and garbled. John stayed in a hospital for ten days, after which Elaine tried to nurse him back to health. During the next few weeks, she watched him carefully and refused to let him go out alone. He protested against his lack of freedom. He insisted on writing several short articles for various magazines, starting a new novel, and planning for a cross-country driving tour, all to convince himself and his wife that he was still a vibrant, healthy man. But even John had to admit that he was no longer as young and healthy as he had once been.

CHAPTER EIGHT

THE GOOD LIFE

Some said he nodded and perhaps dozed, for the testimony to his greatness was long and the monotony of his victories continued for many hours . . . And as he dozed and wished to be otherwhere, he heard his deeds exalted beyond recognition.

—*from The Acts of King Arthur and His Noble Knights*[1]

ON NOVEMBER 5, 1959, Steinbeck wrote a letter to Adlai Stevenson describing what he thought was the nation's biggest problem. Americans, he suggested, have "too many THINGS."

"A strange species we are," he continued. "We can stand anything God and Nature can throw at us save only plenty."[2] He had seen the nation survive the worst economic crisis of its history, the Great Depression, but Steinbeck questioned whether the nation would survive the affluence of the mid-fifties. Somehow

Newsday received a copy of the letter and printed it, sparking a debate about whether the country had, in fact, become too wealthy. Steinbeck enjoyed being at the center of controversy again. And the controversy inspired him as he finished his new novel, *The Winter of Our Discontent.*

Ethan Hawley, the novel's main character, clerks at a grocery store in eastern Long Island. Even though his wife wants him to find a job more suitable to his talents and his children pressure him to provide more material comforts, Hawley has neither the drive nor the ruthlessness to succeed in the business world. But then he devises a scheme for regaining control of his life, a scheme requiring that he sacrifice his friends and ignore his own morality. "We have become ranchers without land, commanders without troops, horsemen on foot. We can't survive," Hawley explains as he justifies his actions. "Perhaps that is one reason why the change was taking place in me. I do not want, never have wanted, money for itself. But money is necessary to keep my place in a category I am used to and comfortable in."[3] Hawley allows his desire for money and comfort to change him. He, like the country Steinbeck described in his letter to Stevenson, allows wealth and power to weaken him.

When *The Winter of Our Discontent* appeared in June 1961 some critics, such as Saul Bellow, praised the novel as Steinbeck's best work in years. "Critics who said of [Steinbeck] that he had seen his best days had better tie on their napkins and prepare to eat crow," Bellow wrote.[4] Yet in the summer and fall of 1960, before the book went to press, Steinbeck doubted himself and the novel he had just finished. Intending to reconnect with his audience and prove to himself that he was not too old and sick to work, he planned a driving tour of the United States. He bought a used van and converted the back into a living space much like the rear of the pie wagon he drove among the Okies in the 1930s. And in September, after a powerful hurricane delayed his departure for a few days, John left Long Island for a three-month, coast-to-coast journey. His pet poodle Charley was his only companion. "This trip was just something John had to do," Elaine remembered years later. "And he had to go alone. . . . He wanted to prove to himself that he was not an old man. He could take control of his life, could drive himself, and could learn things again."[5]

Even though Steinbeck enjoyed the companionship of many generous people during the journey, he suffered from loneliness. The man who spent two winters in virtual isolation at Lake Tahoe now missed his wife and the comforts of home. Elaine caught up with him several times by plane and even traveled with him from Seattle to San Francisco. But these welcome meetings only made their time apart more painful for John. He learned now that he could not push himself the way he had in the past. He rushed through the tour, seeing only a fraction of what he had hoped to see, and returned to the East Coast in time to accompany Elaine to the inauguration of the nation's young, glamorous new president, John F. Kennedy.

In the early winter of 1961, the Steinbecks vacationed in Barbados, where John composed his cross-country account, *Travels with Charley.* When they returned to New York in March, they found Thom and Catbird sitting on the front steps of their house. The boys had argued with Gwyn and run away from home. John and Elaine took the boys in, but John could not address all of their concerns immediately. He was headed to the Pacific to work on another scientific expedition. He flew to San Diego to take his place on a drilling barge, *Cuss I.*, which left the California coast in late March to collect rock samples from the seafloor. Steinbeck acted as project historian, recording the events of the expedition. But he could not enjoy the trip as much as he had hoped; he was too concerned about his sons.

By midsummer, he decided on a way to improve the boys' education and outlook: he took them on a tour of the world. On September 8, John, Elaine, seventeen-year-old Thom, fifteen-year-old Catbird, and Terrence McNally, a young Irish scholar and future playwright acting as the boys' tutor, set sail for England. John planned to lead his boys across Europe and the Middle East, into Asia, and south to Australia. But the plan proved more difficult to enact than John had imagined. First, he had not finished *Travels with Charley*, a book he now called a "formless, shapeless, aimless thing."[6] And when *Holiday* magazine published advance excerpts to popular acclaim, he felt even more pressure to finish the manuscript. But his sons were his real problem in the early fall of 1961. Thom and Catbird rebelled against both McNally's lessons and John's authority and fought each other constantly. After one particularly angry exchange during a stopover in Milan, John retreated to his hotel room, where he suffered yet another stroke. Thom quickly revived his unconscious father, but everyone now agreed that the trip was too stressful for the aging writer.

Refusing to end the trip early, John insisted that the boys continue their tour through Italy, while he and Elaine settled in Capri. McNally and the boys organized

The Steinbeck family posed for this photograph during their 1961 world tour.

smaller excursions, giving John time to recuperate. On February 27, 1962, he turned sixty years old. Physically, he seemed much older. But by the spring, he felt well enough to accompany his sons through southern Italy and Greece, where he discovered that his books were still popular and widely read. And his sons displayed some evidence that they had learned something about the world and that the trip was not a failure. In late May, believing the trip had been a moderate success, Steinbeck canceled the rest of the journey and returned to Sag Harbor.

That summer, Viking published *Travels with Charley* to strong reviews. On the heels of *The Winter of Our Discontent,* the new book suggested that Steinbeck had rediscovered his voice. But Steinbeck feared he was running out of time and energy and that he would not be writing many more books. He announced that he would limit his production in the coming year and reevaluate his career. Pat Covici, as always, tried to preserve his star writer's confidence. "After middle age," he wrote to Steinbeck, "most of us experience and suffer a great change, but often we also experience a new birth. . . . The fact that you mean to do some long slow thinking is proof that there are many more fish in your sea."[7] Despite Covici's optimism, Steinbeck was starting to believe that his career was over.

Just as he considered giving up, however, he received the news he had been waiting for, patiently, for almost twenty years: he had won the Nobel Prize. He was listening to radio reports of the Cuban Missile Crisis on October 24, concerned that the United States and the Soviet Union might go to war in the Caribbean, when a commentator interrupted the broadcast to announce that Steinbeck had won the most prestigious award in world literature. He and Elaine sped to Manhattan later that day to attend a press conference. But, as always, Steinbeck's critics managed to dampen at least some of his joy. The *New York Times* ran an editorial criticizing the Swedish Academy for bestowing the honor on Steinbeck. "Without detracting in the least from Mr. Steinbeck's accomplishments," the editors remarked, "we think it interesting that the laurel was not awarded to a writer—perhaps a poet or critic or historian—whose significance, influence and sheer body of work had already made a more profound impression on the literature of our age."[8] Other newspapers and magazines echoed this criticism; Steinbeck, they suggested, was an old-fashioned writer, irrelevant in the United States of the 1960s. But these critics ignored the fact that Steinbeck remained an immensely popular writer at home and abroad. At the award ceremony in Sweden in early December, the secretary of the Swedish Academy acknowledged John's international stature as well as the special qualities that made his work so valuable:

> *You are not a stranger to the Swedish public any more than to that of your own country and of the whole world. With your most distinctive works you have become a teacher of goodwill and charity, a defender of human values, which can well be said to correspond to the proper idea of the Nobel Prize.*[9]

Warming to such praise, Steinbeck delivered a short speech in which he expressed his belief in the power of literature to change people's lives. Privately, however, he worried that the prize would mark the glorious but premature end of his career.

Home from Sweden in early 1963, John struggled to fulfill the demands placed on a Nobel laureate—public appearances, parties, interviews. He seldom found the time or the energy to write anything for himself. Eye surgery in early May, and a subsequent period of semi-blindness, did not help matters. By the fall, as the Nobel excitement faded and his eyesight returned, he cast about for a new project. Luckily, President Kennedy called on him to undertake a special diplomatic mission. Kennedy asked Steinbeck and young playwright Edward Albee to visit the Soviet Union, contact Soviet writers and students, and explain what life was like in the United States. Steinbeck, knowing that his gruff manner and plainspoken delivery would make enemies in the Soviet Union, hesitated before accepting Kennedy's proposal. "I hope you don't mind if I kick up some dirt while I'm there?" he asked the president. "I expect you to," Kennedy responded.[10] Now, after thirty years of false accusations linking Steinbeck to Communist organizations, a U.S. president asked John Steinbeck to represent the nation to the most powerful Communist country in the world.

Soviet officials greeted the U.S. writers coldly when they landed in Moscow. Spies followed Steinbeck and Albee during most of their travels and harassed them during press conferences and social engagements. The two Americans were forced to conduct secret meetings with student groups and writers whom the Soviet government considered dangerous. But Steinbeck was delighted to find that the Soviet people knew his work. And he surprised them with stories about his freedom as a writer in the United States. When asked why he criticized his own nation in his novels—something the Soviet government prohibited—Steinbeck replied, "Because I love it. If I did not, I would not bother."[11]

Steinbeck and Albee kept a hectic schedule during their stay in the Soviet Union. Steinbeck worked so hard that he collapsed from exhaustion in early November. Ignoring doctors' suggestions that he curtail his trip, he continued to visit with students and intellectuals. In the middle of the month, he and Elaine visited Soviet-dominated Poland and received a hero's welcome. But the trip took on a very different character on November 22, 1963, when the Steinbecks received news of a tragedy back home: President Kennedy had been assassinated. As more details of the assassination reached Europe, distraught Poles visited the U.S. embassy to present Steinbeck with flowers and tributes for his fallen president. The U.S. State Department then asked Elaine and John to visit memorial services held for Kennedy in Vienna and, later, in Budapest, Prague, and West Germany. Originally visiting Europe as a representative of the Kennedy administration, Steinbeck became a central figure in Europe's efforts to remember Kennedy's legacy.

In mid-December, the Steinbecks visited the nation's new president, Lyndon Baines Johnson, to report on their trip through the Soviet Union. Steinbeck and Johnson liked each other immediately, while Elaine and Lady Bird Johnson, both graduates of the University of Texas, reminisced about their college experiences. The Steinbecks would visit the Johnsons frequently in the coming years. In 1964, Johnson presented Steinbeck with the Presidential Medal of Freedom. Later, the president asked Steinbeck for help on his 1964 inaugural address. Meanwhile, in his new role as a government insider, Steinbeck continued to correspond with the Kennedys

John Steinbeck is welcomed to the White House by President Lyndon B. Johnson and his wife Lady Bird.

as well. Former First Lady Jacqueline Kennedy even asked John to write a biography of her husband. Though flattered, Steinbeck declined.

But even if John traveled in important circles in the mid-sixties, the pace of his life slowed considerably. For a short time, he worked on a series of essays for a book of photographs, later published as *America and the Americans.* But he spent more of his time organizing community events in Sag Harbor. He hesitated to begin any new ventures even as Pat Covici begged him for new fiction. "If I have any more work in me, which I sometimes doubt, it will have to be of a kind to match my present age," he wrote in the summer of 1964. "I'm not the young writer of promise any more. I'm a worked-over claim."[12] Pat Covici—John's friend, editor, and confidante—died a few months later, the first in a string of deaths (including Adlai Stevenson and John's younger sister Mary, both of whom died in 1965) that devastated the writer.

Over the next few years, Steinbeck wrote a series of articles for *Newsday*. The newspaper's editors gave him the freedom to explore whatever topics interested him. It was the perfect job for a man who no longer had the patience or discipline to sculpt his ideas into a long literary work. In the winter of 1966, the editors asked Steinbeck to visit Israel and write about what he saw. He and Elaine toured the Holy Land using the Bible as a guidebook. They visited Jerusalem, Tel Aviv, the Dead Sea, and Masada, and John wrote a series of columns praising the energy of the young nation. The trip also took his mind off his failed attempts to write new fiction. He had planned several new works, but none could hold his attention.

Despite his limited output since the publication of *Travels with Charley*, Steinbeck continued to garner national attention as a newspaper columnist and as a Johnson appointee to the National Endowment for the Arts. In the late sixties, as Johnson continued to wage an unpopular war in Vietnam, Steinbeck became one of the few writers or artists who associated with the White House. Torn between his distaste for the war effort and his deep-rooted respect for the presidency,

John Steinbeck toured Vietnam unrestricted by South Vietnam officials.

Steinbeck did not know how to protest the war, preserve his friendship with Johnson, and express his love for the United States. He respected and supported his son Catbird's decision to enlist in the army and join the war effort, but he refused Johnson's request to act as a presidential emissary in Vietnam. Secretly, he hoped to visit Vietnam as an independent reporter, and in late 1966, *Newsday* gave him the opportunity for which he had been waiting.

He and Elaine joined the press corps living in the Caravelle Hotel in Saigon, the capital of South Vietnam. Similar to his travels with Charley, John accepted the war assignment to challenge himself and test his aging body. He traveled in transport planes and helicopters, followed troops into battle, observed Marine maneuvers, and even took courses in weapons operation. Typically, Elaine stayed in Saigon, attending government press briefings and taking notes for her husband. On a few occasions, she even accompanied him to the battle lines. The press captured photos of John crawling through rice paddies with the troops, wearing fatigues and a helmet. When the photos ran in newspapers back home, people who once trusted Steinbeck's judgment came to believe that he supported Johnson's war efforts. And Steinbeck's wartime dispatches reinforced their assumptions, as he praised the heroism of U.S. troops and criticized war protestors in Washington. "Can you understand the quick glow of pride one feels in just belonging to the same species as these men?" he wrote in one positive description of the soldiers. "I suppose it is the opposite of the shiver of shame I sometimes feel at home when I see the [protestors], dirty clothes, dirty minds, sour smelling wastelings."[13] But such passages expressed only part of what Steinbeck felt about the war. He had heard from Catbird that conditions in Vietnam were worse than the government reported, and he now observed wartime atrocities for himself. Soon, he retreated from the war effort entirely. He never criticized his friend Johnson publicly but, after collapsing from exhaustion in February 1967 and returning home, he simply stopped writing about the war.

Suffering the effects of a back injury in mid-October, Steinbeck underwent surgery at New York University Hospital in Manhattan. While he recuperated, he learned that Catbird had been arrested for drug possession while researching an article about the spread of narcotics in the U.S. Army. Catbird was probably innocent. Army officials had already tried to stop him from reporting the scandalous story, and may have attempted to blackmail him. A jury acquitted him during his trial in Washington, DC, in December. But, while Steinbeck supported his son throughout the proceedings, the strain of the trial took its toll on Steinbeck's health.

In late May 1968, after he lost consciousness in the Sag Harbor house, Elaine rushed him to Southampton Hospital. In July, he returned to New York University Hospital after suffering a heart attack. Once an angry, uncooperative patient, he soon became a favorite of the hospital's nurses. The tough-talking writer had mellowed into a charming old man.[14] In Sag Harbor in November, he received guests and watched television shows, often turning down the volume so that he could amuse himself by making up his own dialogue. But the heart attack and strokes had weakened him consider-

The house at Sag Harbor where John Steinbeck spent his final years

ably, as had other health problems such as emphysema and arteriosclerosis. Elaine labored to make him comfortable and was at his side when he died on December 20, 1968.

Hundreds of people attended John's funeral at St. James Episcopal Church in Manhattan. Actor Henry Fonda read some of John's favorite poems during the ceremony. Elaine returned to their Manhattan house that night and placed John's ashes in the backyard garden. In May 1969, Elaine, Thom, and Catbird carried the ashes across the nation to the Garden of Memories Cemetery in Salinas, California, in the region forever known as Steinbeck Country.

Since John Steinbeck's death, Elaine has devoted much of her life to preserving his legacy. Although he burned many of the manuscripts he could not publish, he left a few behind for fans and literary scholars. In 1969, Elaine approved the publication of *Journal of a Novel*, a copy of the journal Steinbeck kept while completing *East of Eden*. In 1975, she and Robert Wallsten edited a volume of Steinbeck's correspondence, *Steinbeck: A Life in Letters*. The next year, she released *The Acts of King Arthur and His Noble Knights*, the translation of Thomas Malory that caused Steinbeck so much distress and pleasure in the later years of his life. And in 1989, Elaine published *Working Days*, the private journals Steinbeck kept while writing *The Grapes of Wrath*.

These posthumous volumes help complete the portrait of Steinbeck as a man who cared deeply about his work and struggled throughout his life to make himself a better writer. But they are only supplements to the vast and varied body of writing Steinbeck left behind. Several of his books—*Of Mice and Men*, *The Pearl*, *The Red Pony* and, to a lesser degree, *Tortilla Flat* and *Cannery Row*—remain important texts on many junior high school and high school reading lists. Others, such as *In Dubious Battle*, *East of Eden*, and *The Winter of Our Discontent* continue to find enthusiastic adult audiences. Steinbeck's work has been translated into more than forty languages and most of his books remain in print.[15] Unlike several of his more famous peers, including Ernest Hemingway, William Faulkner, and F.

Scott Fitzgerald, Steinbeck enjoyed considerable success in Hollywood; his novels and scripts inspired several first-rate motion pictures. Movies based on Steinbeck's work have received twenty-five Oscar nominations and four Academy Awards. Movie studios continue to produce new adaptations of the novels for network and cable television as well as the stage.

Of all Steinbeck's work, however, no book will ever be as important to his reputation as *The Grapes of Wrath.* Still selling almost 50,000 copies each year, *The Grapes of Wrath* is Steinbeck's gift to literary history. During the Great Depression, it provided a cast of mythical characters—Tom Joad, Ma Joad, Jim Casey—who helped the American people understand their own lives. Popular, folk, and political culture absorbed the novel almost immediately. Director John Ford and actor Henry Fonda transformed it into one of the most important films in cinema history. Folksinger Woody Guthrie included a song called "Tom Joad" on his influential 1940 album *Dust Bowl Ballads.* And First Lady Eleanor Roosevelt frequently referred to the novel during her efforts to combat the effects of the Southwestern drought.

Later, as the nation climbed out of the Depression, *The Grapes of Wrath* came to symbolize the effects of poverty more generally and the efforts of common people to maintain their dignity despite intense suffering. In this form, the novel remains an integral part of popular culture. In 1996, rock musician Bruce Springsteen won a Grammy Award for *The Ghost of Tom Joad,* a collection of songs devoted to the plight of the poor and dispossessed in the United States. For his dedication to the American underprivileged, The *New York Times* called Springsteen "Steinbeck in leather."[16] Through such references, Steinbeck's legacy has been preserved. Influenced by *The Grapes of Wrath*, the world continues to associate Steinbeck with the struggles of the poor and lonely.

In *East of Eden*, Steinbeck outlined his criteria for personal success, describing a man who "made many errors in performance but whose effective life was devoted to making men brave and dignified and good in a time when they were poor and frightened and when ugly forces were loose in the world to utilize their fears"[17] According to his own criteria, then, John Steinbeck lived a successful life.

SOURCE NOTES

INTRODUCTION

1. John Steinbeck, *The Acts of King Arthur and His Noble Knights.* (New York: The Noonday Press, 1976), p. 220.
2. John Steinbeck, *Steinbeck: A Life in Letters,* eds. Elaine Steinbeck and Robert Wallsten. (New York: Penguin Books, 1975), p. 897.
3. Herbert Kretzmer, "London Looks at a Durable Giant" (1965) in Thomas Fensch, ed. *Conversations with John Steinbeck.* (Jackson: University Press of Mississippi, 1988), p. 94.

CHAPTER 1

1. *The Acts of King Arthur and His Noble Knights,* p. 176.
2. John Steinbeck, *Journal of a Novel: The* East of Eden *Letters* (New York: Penguin Books, 1969), p. 103.
3. Jay Parini, *John Steinbeck: A Biography* (New York: Henry Holt and Company, 1995), p. 13.
4. *Ibid.*, p. 12.
5. Robert DeMott, introduction to John Steinbeck, *To a God Unknown* (New York: Penguin Books, 1995), p. vii.
6. Parini, pp. 20–21.
7. Jackson J. Benson, *The True Adventures of John*

Steinbeck, Writer (New York: Penguin Books, 1984), p. 43.
8. Parini, p. 37.

CHAPTER 2

1. *The Acts of King Arthur and His Noble Knights,* p. 44.
2. Parini, p. 49.
3. Benson, p. 90.
4. *Steinbeck: A Life in Letters,* p. 3.
5. Parini, p. 63.
6. *Steinbeck: A Life in Letters,* p. 11.
7. Benson, p. 160.
8. *Ibid.*, p. 155.
9. *Steinbeck: A Life in Letters,* p. 15.
10. Benson, 465.
11. *Ibid.*, p. 156.
12. *Steinbeck: A Life in Letters,* p. 32.
13. *Ibid.*, p. 76.
14. James Nagel, introduction to John Steinbeck, *The Pastures of Heaven* (New York: Penguin Books, 1995), pp. xii–xiii.
15. *The Pastures of Heaven,* p. 201.

CHAPTER 3

1. *The Acts of King Arthur and His Noble Knights,* p. 267.
2. *Steinbeck: A Life in Letters,* p. 87.
3. Parini, p. 182.
4. *Ibid.*, p. 148-49.
5. John Steinbeck, *In Dubious Battle* (New York: Penguin Books, 1992), p. 16.
6. *Steinbeck: A Life in Letters,* p. 110.
7. John Steinbeck, *Tortilla Flat* (New York: Penguin Books, 1986), p. 2.

8. Ella Winter, "Sketching the Author of *Tortilla Flat*" (1935) in Fensch, p. 3.
9. *Steinbeck: A Life in Letters,* p. 111.
10. Benson, p. 335.
11. John Steinbeck, *Of Mice and Men* (New York: Penguin Books, 1993), p. 57.
12. *New York World Telegram,* "More a Mouse Than a Man, Steinbeck Faces Reporters" (1937) in Fensch, p. 6.
13. Parini, p. 191–92.
14. *Ibid.,* p. 195.

CHAPTER 4

1. *The Acts of King Arthur and His Noble Knights,* p. 251.
2. John Steinbeck, *Working Days: The Journals of* The Grapes of Wrath, ed. Robert DeMott (New York: Penguin Books, 1989), p. 26.
3. Parini, p. 202.
4. John H. Timmerman, introduction to John Steinbeck, *The Long Valley* (New York: Penguin Books, 1995), p. xx.
5. *Steinbeck: A Life in Letters,* p. 173.
6. *Ibid.,* p. 178.
7. John Steinbeck, *The Grapes of Wrath* (New York: Penguin Books, 1986), p. 449.
8. *Ibid.,* p. 31.
9. *Ibid.,* p. 537.
10. Benson, p. 422.
11. *Steinbeck: A Life in Letters,* p. 138.
12. Charles Wollenberg, introduction to John Steinbeck, *The Harvest Gypsies: On the Road to the Grapes of Wrath* (Berkeley: Heyday Books, 1988), p. xiv.
13. Benson, p. 445.

14. *Steinbeck: A Life in Letters*, p. 206.
15. *Ibid.*, p. 227.
16. Donald V. Coers, introduction to John Steinbeck, *The Moon is Down* (New York: Penguin Books, 1995), p. xi.
17. *The Moon is Down*, p. 19.
18. Coers, xii.
19. *Ibid.*, xii.
20. *Steinbeck: A Life in Letters*, p. 244.

CHAPTER 5

1. *The Acts of King Arthur and His Noble Knights*, p. 129.
2. Robert E. Morsberger, "Steinbeck's Screenplays and Productions" in John Steinbeck, *Zapata* (New York: Penguin Books, 1991), p. 344.
3. Parini, p. 272.
4. John Steinbeck, *Once There Was a War* (New York: Penguin Books, 1994), p. 151.
5. Benson, p. 532.
6. Parini, p. 278.
7. Richard Astro, introduction to John Steinbeck, *The Log from the Sea of Cortez* (New York: Penguin Books, 1995), p. viii.
8. *Steinbeck: A Life in Letters*, pp. 272–73.
9. John Steinbeck, *Cannery Row* (New York: Penguin Books, 1992), p. 141.
10. Parini, p. 286.
11. *Steinbeck: A Life in Letters*, pp. 280–81.
12. Benson, p. 572.

CHAPTER 6

1. *The Acts of King Arthur and His Noble Knights*, p. 280.
2. *Steinbeck: A Life in Letters*, p. 293.

3. Benson, p. 586.
4. Coers, p. xxiii.
5. John Steinbeck, *A Russian Journal* (New York: The Viking Press, 1948), p. 220.
6. *Steinbeck: A Life in Letters*, p. 310.
7. Parini, p. 323.
8. *Steinbeck: A Life in Letters*, p. 312.
9. *Ibid.*, p. 339.
10. Benson, p. 637.
11. *Zapata*, p. 141.
12. *Steinbeck: A Life in Letters*, p. 344.
13. Parini, p. 332.
14. *Steinbeck: A Life in Letters*, p. 356.
15. *Ibid.*, p. 354.
16. *Zapata*, p. 297.
17. Parini, p. 342.

CHAPTER 7

1. *The Acts of King Arthur and His Noble Knights*, p. 31.
2. John Steinbeck, *East of Eden* (New York: Penguin Books, 1992), preface.
3. *Journal of a Novel*, p. 4.
4. *East of Eden*, p. 570.
5. *Ibid., p.* 303.
6. Parini, pp. 361–62.
7. John Steinbeck, *Sweet Thursday* (New York: Penguin Books, 1996), p. 260.
8. *Steinbeck: A Life in Letters*, p. 497.
9. *Ibid.*, p. 516.
10. Parini, p. 394.
11. *The Acts of King Arthur and His Noble Knights*, p. xii.
12. *Steinbeck: A Life in Letters*, p. 609.
13. *Ibid.*, p. 627.

CHAPTER 8

1. *The Acts of King Arthur and His Noble Knights*, p. 286.
2. *Steinbeck: A Life in Letters*, p. 152.
3. John Steinbeck, *The Winter of Our Discontent* (New York: Penguin Books, 1996), p. 104.
4. Parini, p. 431.
5. *Ibid.*, pp. 419–20.
6. *Steinbeck: A Life in Letters*, p. 702.
7. Parini, p. 443.
8. *Ibid.*, p. 445.
9. Benson, p. 919.
10. Parini, p. 451.
11. Benson, p. 932.
12. *Steinbeck: A Life in Letters*, p. 802.
13. Benson, p. 1000.
14. *Ibid.*, p. 1029.
15. Parini, p. xiv.
16. *New York Times Magazine*, June 26, 1997, front cover.
17. *East of Eden*, p. 414.

FOR MORE INFORMATION

BIOGRAPHIES

Benson, Jackson J. *The True Adventures of John Steinbeck, Writer.* New York: Penguin Books, 1984.

Parini, Jay. *John Steinbeck: A Biography.* New York: Henry Holt and Company, 1995.

LETTERS, JOURNALS, ESSAYS

Fensch, Thomas, ed. *Conversations with John Steinbeck.* Jackson: University Press of Mississippi, 1988.

Steinbeck, John. *Journal of a Novel: The* East of Eden *Letters.* New York: Penguin Books, 1969.

Steinbeck: A Life in Letters, eds. Elaine Steinbeck and Robert Wallsten. New York: Penguin Books, 1975.

Working Days: The Journals of The Grapes of Wrath, ed. Robert DeMott. New York: Penguin Books, 1989.

Wyatt, David, ed. *New Essays on* The Grapes of Wrath. New York: Cambridge University Press, 1990.

FICTION BY JOHN STEINBECK

Penguin Books has reprinted all of Steinbeck's fiction in paperback editions. Some editions include helpful introductory essays by prominent scholars of Steinbeck's work.

Cup of Gold, 1929.
Pastures of Heaven, 1932.
*To a God Unknown,*1933.
Tortilla Flat, 1935.
In Dubious Battle, 1936.
Of Mice and Men, 1937.
The Red Pony, 1937.
The Long Valley, 1938.
The Grapes of Wrath, 1939.
The Moon is Down, 1942.
Cannery Row, 1945.
The Wayward Bus, 1947.
*The Pearl,*1947.
Burning Bright, 1950.
East of Eden, 1952.
Sweet Thursday, 1954.
The Short Reign of Pippin IV, 1957.
The Winter of Our Discontent, 1961.
The Acts of King Arthur and His Noble Knights. New York: The Noonday Press, 1976.

NONFICTION BY JOHN STEINBECK

Included here are the editions cited in this biography. Some of Steinbeck's nonfiction works have been reprinted. Others can be found only in libraries and bookstores that sell used books.

The Harvest Gypsies: On the Road to The Grapes of Wrath. Berkeley: Heyday Books, 1988. (A collection of the articles Steinbeck wrote for the *San Francisco News*, originally collected in 1938 under the title *Their Blood is Strong*.)

Ricketts, Edward F. and John Steinbeck. *Sea of Cortez: A Leisurely Journal of Travel and Research*. New York: The Viking Press, 1941.

The Forgotten Village. New York: The Viking Press, 1941. (A companion to the documentary of the same name.)

Bombs Away: The Story of a Bomber Team. New York: The Viking Press, 1942.

A Russian Journal. New York: The Viking Press, 1948.

The Log from the Sea of Cortez. New York: Penguin Books, 1951.

Once There Was a War. New York: Penguin Books, 1958. (A collection of Steinbeck's World War II dispatches.)

Travels with Charley in Search of America. New York: Book-of-the-Month Club, 1962.

America and Americans. New York: The Viking Press, 1966.

Zapata. New York: Penguin Books, 1975. (This volume contains introductory essays, Steinbeck's original manuscript on the life of Emiliano Zapata, and the final screenplay of *Viva Zapata!*)

STEINBECK FILMS

This list includes only film adaptations produced by major Hollywood studios.

Of Mice and Men, United Artists, 1939.
The Grapes of Wrath, Twentieth Century-Fox, 1940.
Tortilla Flat, MGM, 1942.
The Moon is Down, Twentieth Century-Fox, 1943.
Lifeboat, Twentieth Century-Fox, 1944.
A Medal for Benny, Paramount, 1945.
The Pearl, RKO, 1948.
The Red Pony, Republic, 1949.
Viva Zapata! Twentieth Century-Fox, 1952.
East of Eden, Warner Bros., 1955.
The Wayward Bus, Twentieth Century-Fox, 1957.
Cannery Row, MGM, 1982.

WEB SITES

The Access Indiana Teaching & Learning Center's John Steinbeck page:
http://tlc.ai.org/steinbec.htm

John Steinbeck's Pacific Grove:
http://www.93950.com/steinbeck/

Monterey County Historical Society:
http://users.dedot.com/mchs/

The National Steinbeck Center:
http://www.steinbeck.org/homepage.html

San Jose State University Center for Steinbeck Studies:
http://www.sjsu.edu/depts/steinbec/srchome.html

INDEX

ABOUT THE AUTHOR

JOHN TESSITORE, a former editor of Maxim magazine, is currently pursuing his doctorate in American Studies at Boston University. He has written biographies of Ernest Hemingway, Muhammad Ali, and Kofi Annan, all for Franklin Watts.